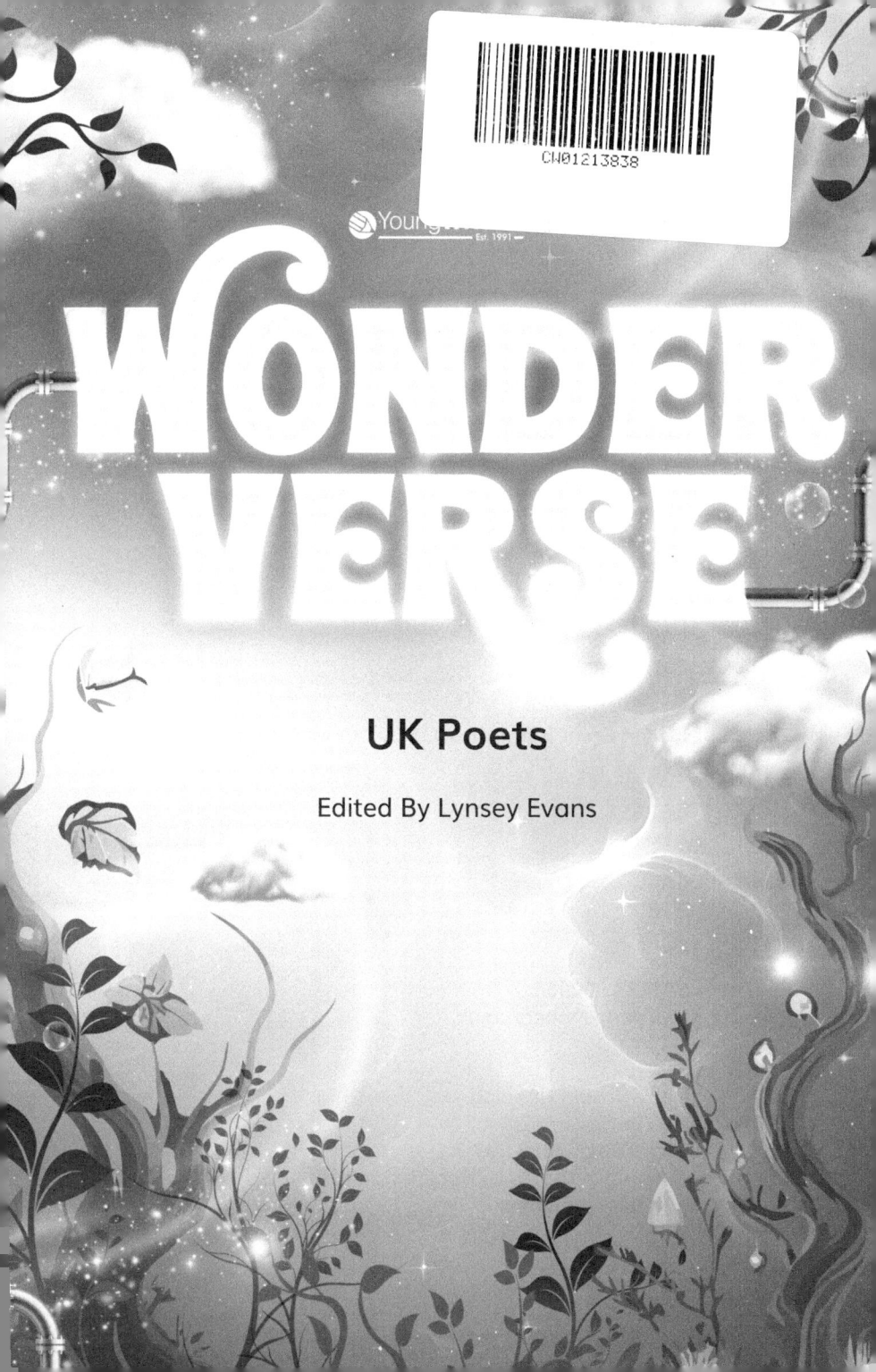

WONDER VERSE

UK Poets

Edited By Lynsey Evans

First published in Great Britain in 2025 by:

![Young Writers Est. 1991]

Young Writers
Remus House
Coltsfoot Drive
Peterborough
PE2 9BF
Telephone: 01733 890066
Website: www.youngwriters.co.uk

All Rights Reserved
Book Design by Davina Hopping
© Copyright Contributors 2024
Softback ISBN 978-1-83685-097-7
Printed and bound in the UK by BookPrintingUK
Website: www.bookprintinguk.com
YB0622N

FOREWORD

WELCOME READER,

For Young Writers' latest competition *Wonderverse*, we asked primary school pupils to explore their creativity and write a poem on any topic that inspired them. They rose to the challenge magnificently with some going even further and writing stories too! The result is this fantastic collection of writing in a variety of styles.

Here at Young Writers our aim is to encourage creativity in children and to inspire a love of the written word, so it's great to get such an amazing response, with some absolutely fantastic pieces. This open theme of this competition allowed them to write freely about something they are interested in, which we know helps to engage kids and get them writing. Within these pages you'll find a variety of topics, from hopes, fears and dreams, to favourite things and worlds of imagination. The result is a collection of brilliant writing that showcases the creativity and writing ability of the next generation.

I'd like to congratulate all the young writers in this anthology, I hope this inspires them to continue with their creative writing.

CONTENTS

Bantock Primary School, Pennfields

Casey Ebeso (8)	1
Owens (8)	2
Japji Aujla (8)	3

Barnham Broom CE (VA) Primary School, Barnham Broom

Johan Sunil (10)	4
Elliott Weston (11)	5
Willow Hoey (11)	6
Jasmine Day (10)	7
Joshua Sunil (10)	8
Phoebe Weston (9)	9
Emily Chester (9)	10
Sofia Hubbard (10)	11

Birchills CE Community Academy, Walsall

Rachel Mikelko (8)	12
Rahima Akther (9)	14
Faith Azeez (8)	15
Somma Okafor (8)	16
Kandil-Fatimah Karim (8)	17

Brookvale Primary School, Erdington

Ashiya Rawlins (8)	18
William Kayes (8)	19
Alaia-Mai Eardley (7)	20
Estelle Scott (9)	21
Abdul-Ahad Qasim (9)	22
Penelope Earls (9)	23

Ava Henry (10)	24
Aneesah Tanai (7)	25
Emma N (8)	26
Dawud Bukhari (7)	27
Ayva Howe (9)	28
Zaroon Rizwan (10)	29
Isabelle Merchant (9)	30
Zaid Ali (9)	31
Ariya Patel (7)	32
Asiya Hannah Khan (8)	33
Warren Y (10)	34
Aarav Verma (7)	35

Harris Academy Tottenham, London

Vanessa Solyga (9)	36
Maryam Harrou (9)	38
Timilehin Olusomoka (9)	39
Farida Mostafa (9)	40
Naylaa Shaik (9)	41
Abby Toska (9)	42
Jude Royles (10)	43

Houghton-On-The-Hill Church Of England Primary School, Houghton On The Hill

Harriet Thomas (9)	44
Penelope Cadman (9)	45
Pavan Manak (9)	46
Poppy Line (9)	47
Eemia Popat (9)	48
Faye Kingham (10)	49

Norwich Road Academy, Thetford

Julia Ratajczak (9)	50
Manna Santhosh (9)	52
Afrin Aara (10)	53
Ariella Wood (10)	54
Samantha Tucker (10)	55
Vihaan Tirumalasetty (10)	56
Teja Zinkeviciute (10)	57
Penelope Ffitch (10)	58

Outwoods Edge Primary School, Loughborough

Saxon Edwards (9)	59
Anaiya Noghan (10)	60
Lily Brennan (7)	62
Amy D'Oyly-Watkins (8)	63
Freya Butler (10)	64
Sienna Musson (9)	65
Lyla Walker (9)	66
Aleena Sudhan (8)	67
Ryan Midzi (8)	68
Thomas Porter (8)	69
Zlata Dimitrova (10)	70
Courtney-Leigh Holland (9)	71
Loki MacTavish (7)	72
Sophie Killick (10)	73
Jaxon Bryans (8)	74
Tishya Miglani (9)	75
Emilie Garvin (7)	76
Bella Bennion (9)	77
Rory Ward (7)	78
Petr Borisov (7)	79
Evie Headley (10)	80
Emily Russell (8)	81
Oscar McGowan (9)	82
Sienna Hall (9)	83
Amelia Smith (8)	84
Imogen Lane (9)	85
Louis Dale (7)	86
Jamie Hicks (8)	87
Esme Maden (9)	88
Violet Dale (10)	89
Adam Howe (9)	90
Beth Gardner (8)	91

Pelham Primary School, London

Chisom Chinedu (7)	92
Sofiia Khoteeva (7)	93
Brody Watson (9)	94
Evie Johnson (9)	95
Xavier Phillip-Andrew (8)	96
Marwa Khan (8)	97
Sunu Park (8)	98
Cassia Reed (9)	99
Dayeon Lee (7)	100
Penelope Buchanan (7)	101
Ether Cobblah (9)	102
Ayda Byrne (7)	103
Sofia Rigoli (7)	104
Matilda Packwood (7)	105
Olivia Mannion (9)	106
Sara Nandagopal (8)	107
Mariam Choudhury (7)	108
Safa Khan (7)	109
Lía Sánchez Conesa (7)	110
Harper Gregorowski (8)	111
Bethany Bartlett (8)	112
Manuel Tranquilli (7)	113
Giorgia Davis (9)	114
Alice Berry (9)	115
Tomas Ferreira Fernandes (7)	116
Avi Daren (8)	117
Alice Aldridge (7)	118
Giselle So (8)	119
Clemmie Cullen (9)	120
Emily Wolman (8)	121
Henry Barnes (8)	122
Kiara Nandagopal (8)	123
Fred Paton (7)	124

Saxon Way Primary School, Gillingham

Ellie Jones (9)	125

Olivia Mclaren (9)	126
Dylan Sterling (10)	128
Aleeza Nouman (9)	129
Ollie Gaydon	130
Esther Akinyemi (10)	131
Shambhavi Gupta (10)	132
Kameelah Oladipupo (9)	133
Sofia Kennerley (9)	134
Sydney Dimond (10)	135
Iretemide Lawal (10)	136
Tekena Clark (9)	137
Tochi Ifeanyi (10)	138
Nassir Popoola (9)	139
Uwakmfon Nelson (9)	140
Hannah Stevens (9)	141
Leyton Michael Adams (9)	142
Abdulgaffar Mustrapha (9)	143
Scarlett East (9)	144
Chimebuka Elekwachi (9)	145
Kitty Collingwood-Taylor (9)	146
Alex	147

St Thomas More Catholic Voluntary Academy, Leicester

Matilda Simpson (8)	148
Elodie Phythian (9)	150
Zahra Hassan (9)	151
Irene Riganello (8)	152
William Addison-Smith (10)	153
Tilly Abbott (8)	154
Mayven Gadalla (9)	155
Kristine Joseph (9)	156

St Wilfrid's Catholic Primary School, Angmering

Lottie Foan (9)	157
Ruth Clarke (9)	158
Daragh MacManus (9)	160

Stockwell Primary School, Lambeth

Angela Passos (9)	161
Dylan Tabares Isaza (7)	162
Ayub Mohamud (10)	163
Mellany Angel Vieira (7)	164
Leena Omar Mohammed Ali (9)	165
Leonardo Ferreira (6)	166
Erin Bohan (8)	167
Elijah Shipman (8)	168
Halima Begum (8)	169
Shersy Encarnacion Arias (10)	170
Matilde Correia (8)	171

Temple Sutton Primary School, Southend-On-Sea

Faith Leach (8)	172
Callum Armstrong (8)	174
Dolly Aylott (9)	175
Evelyn-Ivy Poppy Button (9)	176
Lillie Stemp (8)	177
Victoria Ginn (8)	178
Nithika Selvakumar (9)	179
Tola Grabowska (9)	180
Oscar Hainesborough (9)	181
Ajla Malka (9)	182
Sadie Wavell (9)	183
William Smith (8)	184
KC-Mylia Linggood (9)	185
Mia Rouse (9)	186
Habibat Waheed (10)	187
Evie-Rose Muller (8)	188
Ofelia Dean (8)	189
Dominic Smith (10)	190
Vinnie Wright (9)	191
Sienna O'Neill (9)	192
Ria Simpson (9)	193
Kleisa Kaloshi (8)	194
Isabella Jo Ann Lew (8)	195
Sunny Li (8)	196

The New Beacon School, Sevenoaks

Freddie Fletcher (8)	197

Thorpe Primary School, Idle

Isabella Jackson (8)	198
Bella-Mai B (8)	199
Anaya Shah (9)	200
Anishah Eqbal (9)	201
Isabel Waite (8)	202
Natalie Greaves (8)	203

Woodstock Primary School, Leicester

Kaiden Kelly (9)	204
Marlvin Ndlovu (8)	206
Ava Connely (8)	207
Zohaib Shah (8)	208
Beau Mitchell (9)	209
Harvi Parvaga (8)	210
Mya Gregory (8)	211
Freddie Beeching-Townsend (8)	212
Nimrat Kaur (8)	213
Kingsley Baptiste (8)	214
Jaden Tandel (8)	215
Mohammed Sulaimon (8)	216
Mohamed Osman (8)	217
Iman Siyad (8)	218
Paigan Goulty (8)	219
Shevin Geekianage (8)	220
Oscar Smyth (8)	221
Redeen Mahmood (8)	222
Courtney Howkins (8)	223
Bilal Youssouf (8)	224
Anaya Chauhan (9)	225
Skyler Wall-Finnemore (9)	226
Khortez-Azzi Seare (8)	227
Lehat Ibrahim (8)	228
Bentley Thompson (8)	229
Kazirie Morgan (8)	230
Praise Iyobosa Ekhase (8)	231
Star Cassidy (8)	232

THE CREATIVE WRITING

My Family Diary

My sister is very kind,
And she likes a lot of blue,
She always acts like she's the best,
But she always has my back too.

My mum is as confident as a peacock,
She works as fast as a cheetah,
My mum loves food, like bears,
She loves talking with her friends.

My dad is a nice man,
He loves vibing to football,
My dad likes to eat British food,
Like how a predator loves their prey.

My big sister Wendy,
Loves her press-on nails,
She also loves watermelon,
Like a lion likes running.

Casey Ebeso (8)
Bantock Primary School, Pennfields

In The Cage

There was a prison full of cages,
But there were people with different ages.
While the guards were walking,
The prisoners were talking.

One day the fire was lit,
But no one could fit.
He was eating,
While everyone was sleeping.

The pipe was leaking,
But everyone was sleeping.
The floor was flooding,
When they awoke they were all floating.

That day they were free,
Then they played with a Frisbee.
When they were done,
They were alone once more.

Owens (8)
Bantock Primary School, Pennfields

Space

In space there are many satellites
And the sun shines very bright
In space there are lots of stars
Which shine far, far away
In space there are lots of aliens
Playing day and night.

Japji Aujla (8)
Bantock Primary School, Pennfields

A Sunny Friend

I was sitting outside my balcony
The summer breeze tickling my face
Birds were chirping happily
And oak tree leaves danced with grace
The wonderful day was ending
The bright sun was about to set
Birds flew back to their nests
I was wondering where my mum was, when
I heard a sweet voice from above
I looked up, it was the sun!
It asked, "What are you doing, my little friend?"
I said, "Waiting for my mum to come from work."
The sun smiled and stayed a bit longer
Even when it was time to go
I felt like it was giving me company
A few minutes later Mum came home
I ran downstairs to greet her
I waved at the sun and said goodbye
And it sank into the sea to sleep well
The dazzling sun will be back tomorrow
To light up our lives once more
And I will be there on my balcony
To greet my sunny friend.

Johan Sunil (10)
Barnham Broom CE (VA) Primary School, Barnham Broom

Five Wonderful Worlds

As I open the door, what do I see?
A *monstrous* big *blackhole* engulfing me,
It sucks me up, I see the lights,
But it all ends with candy delight,
Clouds of cotton candy, lakes of chocolate custard,
I dare say even I would frown at hot dogs and mustard,
But there I go again, off to a new world,
Where fire bright now swirls,
I walk to a gate and walk some more,
Away from the scorching core,
Into a land where tennis balls are hit,
Where the chorus sings and lights are lit,
And again I go to the shimmering stones,
Underwater worlds, chests bearing crossbones,
I must hold my breath and swim to the top,
To find myself in a book shop,
I take one out and look at a page,
Then realise I'm back to the dinosaur age,
Then *whoosh* I'm off and as I open the door
What do I see?
My bedroom looking glumly back at me.

Elliott Weston (11)
Barnham Broom CE (VA) Primary School, Barnham Broom

The Aura Of Night

As the glorious light fades away,
A candlelit radiance can still stay.
A glowing ember, of no other place,
It is no lamp or torchlight trace:
A glimmer of dreams, hidden in plain sight,
As the benevolent world welcomes the night.
The waves and the tide settle and fade out,
Nightingales take off and to their friends, they shout.
This mesmerising beacon which we can see,
Shall set the world's worries entirely free.
He stays there all night to bring peace to all,
Until the sun's rays of light come to call.
But who is this protector, of all that we know?
Wait until night-time, to see his wondrous glow.

Willow Hoey (11)
Barnham Broom CE (VA) Primary School, Barnham Broom

Rajah

A ginger cat squeaks away
His eyes as wide as saucers
As green as the Amazon
As big and deep as the ocean.

His whiskers as white as snow
As delicate as the finest silk.

His big and padded paws
Silent as can be
With pink toes that match his nose.

His tiger-patterned tail
Stands tall and proud
If you dare spook him
It will turn into a bush.

His fur sleek and soft
Ginger stripes galore!
Strong and powerful but cute and cuddly
He is my ginger fur baby, Rajah.

Jasmine Day (10)
Barnham Broom CE (VA) Primary School, Barnham Broom

Life In Space

I woke up in the middle of the galaxy
Wearing the proper attire of an astronaut
The stars were shining bright
The Earth was very far but the moon was very close
Suddenly a rocket zoomed right past me
I nearly escaped that but something caught my attention
A shooting star launching through the whole galaxy
Immediately one came flying at me and right before it hit me
My mum woke me up and she told me that I was late for school
And asked me to get ready
I realised it was all a dream
But it felt so real.

Joshua Sunil (10)
Barnham Broom CE (VA) Primary School, Barnham Broom

Season's Reading

As winter draws nearer, bitterly cold,
Nature turns dull and trees grow bald,
My body shivers, my feet start to freeze
Then here comes the chill of the cold winter breeze.
But then *whoosh!* Off I go,
I'm quite confused because there is no more snow.
Instead, neat green fields are before my eyes
My body feels warm, I am gifted with the sun's beaming prize.
But I don't have much time to look,
As I fly away into a new book.

Phoebe Weston (9)
Barnham Broom CE (VA) Primary School, Barnham Broom

Friendship

F riends are like jewels
R ubies, sapphires, emeralds
I nvisible at times
E ven though they are there
N o matter where
D espite the distance
S ometimes close, sometimes far
H earing your voice
I nspiring your heart
P erhaps they'll always be there.

Emily Chester (9)
Barnham Broom CE (VA) Primary School, Barnham Broom

Thunderstorm

When the rain comes to stay, lightning roars,
They bring fear upon all,
As people run and hide,
A tornado and whirlpool arrive,
Children crying and screaming,
When suddenly a ray of light comes beaming,
Everyone looks to the light,
Their faces gleaming,
The sun has come,
The storm is gone.

Sofia Hubbard (10)
Barnham Broom CE (VA) Primary School, Barnham Broom

Seasons

Autumn came by
Leaves fell down dramatically
As the sweet wind
Filled the air
People crunched the
Leaves and flakes
Fell to the ground

Winter then came by
Snowflakes fell on the
Ground gently
Snow sprinkled
On the ground
The perfect
Day to have
Hot chocolate
For a cold
Weather
Winter flew by...

Spring buzzed by
Flowers sprang
In the sunshine
Flowers danced

In the sun
Bees buzzed
Around. The bees
Pollinated the flowers
Butterflies fluttered
Around.

Summer came by
Hot weather
For a jump
In the pool
And a glass
Of lemonade
And a hat
Weather for
Making sandcastles.

Rachel Mikelko (8)
Birchills CE Community Academy, Walsall

A Dance Of Wings

Fluttering free in the golden light,
Graceful butterflies take to flight,
Their fragile wings paint the sky,
In hues of colours that mystify.

A dance of wings with elegance,
In nature's ancient, timeless trance,
Through fields of flowers they roam,
Bringing beauty to every home.

Their delicate presence, a sight so rare,
A symbol of transformation beyond compare,
From cocoon to fluttering creature,
They embody nature's gentle feature.

So let us watch in wonder and awe,
As butterflies glide without a flaw,
May their beauty and grace inspire,
As they soar higher and higher.

Rahima Akther (9)
Birchills CE Community Academy, Walsall

The Playground Of Memories

The rolling cup blew my mind because the sight of everything in a revolving world is amazing.
The roundabout was very fast
Many other people pushed it
I became the world's fastest bullet
Splash, the water slide was exhilarating.
For enjoying the splash of water
Like dipping in the world's coldest swimming ocean ever.
I ran to meet the strong cobweb
To feel the sunshine on my face when I reach the top.
The green pitch turns picnic, since I have no ball or boot.
I long to see you again by the weekend afternoon, oh dear park!

Faith Azeez (8)
Birchills CE Community Academy, Walsall

Nature

Nature is beautiful but as you wonder it gets better
We don't want to hurt nature
Or you'll hurt Earth
People try their best
But it's not worth it
As we take care
Earth is saved more
We pray to the lord
So we can be strong
It's like rainbows
It's like a lake
Nature's beauty grows more and more
It shines in the sun
It sways in the breeze
Animals live there
So we take care of these.

Somma Okafor (8)
Birchills CE Community Academy, Walsall

Friendship

A friend is like a star that
Twinkles and glows or maybe
Like an ocean that gently slows
A friend is like gold, that you
Should treasure and take care of
Forever and ever
A friend is like an angel that
Is there to guide you
A friend is someone you can trust
Out of a few
A friend is more than one in
A million
They are one in a zillion
And you, my friend, are very special.

Kandil-Fatimah Karim (8)
Birchills CE Community Academy, Walsall

Special Space

When I grow up, I want to go to space
Space is super
When I'm there, I want to see the active aliens doing their jobs
There might be surprises there and treats
There might be some that I can eat

There is no gravity in space so I will be upside down
I wonder what space food tastes like?
Maybe sweet and soft like cotton candy, who knows?
In space, anything goes!

I will float around all day long and eat doughnuts for breakfast, dinner and dessert
Perhaps chocolate for lunch, that wouldn't hurt
I will fly around the galaxy at 1 million miles per hour
Eating space biscuits, taking space showers!
Laughing with glee, happy as can be
Would you like to come to space with me?

Ashiya Rawlins (8)
Brookvale Primary School, Erdington

The Viking Vibe

If you want to be
A Viking just like me
You must learn our history
I'm a Norseman brave and true
We started exploring close to 802.

We travelled by longboat far and wide
Through stormy seas and riversides
We raided and traded throughout the lands
Our boats were powered by many hands
We found America at least 500 years before
Anyone else thought to explore.

We, the Vikings, have many gods
From Odin the god of war
To the trickster Loki and even Thor
If our warriors die in battle
Off to Valhalla they will go
To feast and celebrate their fallen foe.
Are you a Viking?
Let me see
Of course you are
You talk like me.

William Kayes (8)
Brookvale Primary School, Erdington

Poems Of Seasons

Spring:
I looked outside my window and I saw the plants growing,
But the grass was too long because it needed a good mowing.

Summer:
I went to the beach and it was sandy,
I saw my friend. Her name was Mandi.
We built a sandcastle in the heat,
The sun was hot. It burnt my feet.

Autumn:
When the leaves fall off the trees, it's because of the breeze.
There's a lot of wind and it makes me sneeze.

Winter:
In winter, the nights are cold and filled with ice
I love being cosy, and inside it feels so nice.

Alaia-Mai Eardley (7)
Brookvale Primary School, Erdington

In The Mirror

In the mirror, I see a beautiful, strong girl just like me.
In the mirror, I see an elegant girl drinking tea.
In the mirror, I see a girl twirling around just like me.
In the mirror, I see a girl holding a detailed key.
In the mirror, I see a girl wearing an expensive crown.
I bet she doesn't live in a small town.
In the mirror, I see a girl who looks so fancy.
I think her nickname should be Fancy Nancy.
She lives in the mirror,
In a land
Far, far away that hasn't been found.

Estelle Scott (9)
Brookvale Primary School, Erdington

Future Life!

People fly in planes,
Even if it rains,
People fly in A380s,
Many people buy from JDs,
Have you seen a plane fly?
Or even pass by?
Do you want to fly on a 747?
Maybe when you are eleven?
Have you seen a raven,
Passing by a 747?
If the US have over 19,700 airports,
It should have a lot of sports,
It surely has football,
Have you seen a mall?
Go to a mall,
I mean a shopping centre,
Where you can buy a shower,
For free,
Don't trust me!

Abdul-Ahad Qasim (9)
Brookvale Primary School, Erdington

Candyland

I had a dream of candies and sweets
With gingerbread houses and chocolate-covered streets
Candy cane leaves
Lollipop trees
Anything you have ever wanted you can get with ease
With lemon sherbert bumble bees
And lakes made of honey
The beauty of this paradise is that you don't need any money
All the possible candy
Every single dish
And all you have to do is make one wish
All the drinks are lemonade
This dream will never ever fade.

Penelope Earls (9)
Brookvale Primary School, Erdington

Beyond The Woods

Beyond the dangerous forest
Which is forbidden after dark
Lies two fairy tale schools
Separated yet apart
Connected by a bridge
One school, brave and good
One is nefarious and evil
Getting one chance for your fairy tale
Ever after
Or never after
Princess or witch
Prince or warlock
Slaying dragons or planning evil schemes
Finding true love or losing your dreams
Wherever you go
You always have your friends.

Ava Henry (10)
Brookvale Primary School, Erdington

Emotions

E veryone experiences different emotions
M ondays make me happy as I look forward to the week
O ther days I may feel sad about things
T uesday makes me feel tired as I run around in PE
I feel excited when spending time with my friends
O ut of all emotions, anger is my favourite
N ot knowing how to control my emotions can be confusing
S ome emotions can cause a good day, others a bad day.

Aneesah Tanai (7)
Brookvale Primary School, Erdington

Untitled

Look at autumn bringing out their colours,
Instead of the gloominess we have,
Look at autumn to save the day,
And look at autumn giving you a wave,
Look at autumn, the favourite season of the day,
Who doesn't like it?
That means you're rude today,
Autumn watches you day and night,

For a long time,
With happiness forever and ever,
Autumn, autumn, don't be shy,
Everyone loves you, right?

Emma N (8)
Brookvale Primary School, Erdington

Magical Place

Walking nowhere to be seen
See a magic place
I enter
My dreams are all in a world
It's a sky
Oh my!
How are you?
I see my favourite animal
A dragon
I'm high
Is it all a lie?
Well we'll find out
Let's go in the clouds
Ahh!
Am I dreaming?
This is all my dream
I love this
It's *amazing*
It's like a huge party
I am amazed.

Dawud Bukhari (7)
Brookvale Primary School, Erdington

Friendship

F riends make every day so bright,
R unning and playing from morning to night,
I magining stories big and small,
E very moment is the best of all,
N ever sad, we always smile,
D ancing around in a funny style,
S haring jokes, stories and dreams,
H aving fun with such ease,
I n all our games we say,
"**P** als forever, all the way!"

Ayva Howe (9)
Brookvale Primary School, Erdington

Neil Armstrong

First man on the moon,
A man who changed history forevermore,
Rotating in time and space,
Is indeed a gigantic hurdle,
Humanity has an archive of stuff to explore,
From black holes to giant stars,
So many things to look up,
So much unfounded knowledge,
Everybody wonders if life could be on other planets,
Who doesn't?
So... are we alone in the universe?

Zaroon Rizwan (10)
Brookvale Primary School, Erdington

Nightmare

N ighttime is the place to be
I n dreams is where he will see me
G hosts and ghouls haunt my dreams
H ome is where I want to be
T errified is what you'll be
M ysterious sounds in your dreams
A man in your dream will make you scream
R eady for the terrifying adventure
E vil spirits you will find.

Isabelle Merchant (9)
Brookvale Primary School, Erdington

Candy Country

A world of candy is a great treat indeed,
So come here and see what you can read.
All the candy is yours to eat,
I promise you it does taste sweet.
Lots of houses made from candy,
This place is called Candy Country.
Candy footballs, candy basketballs,
Candy shops and candy malls.
Everything is made from candy,
This place will be very yummy.

Zaid Ali (9)
Brookvale Primary School, Erdington

The Four Seasons

Winter is cold, winter is fun.
You get to spend time with your family.

Next is spring when plants start to sprout,
And a new beginning for lambs and chicks.

Summer is hot, you can play in the pool
And get nice and cool.

Autumn is colourful, leaves start to fall.
Trees are getting ready for winter to start again.

Ariya Patel (7)
Brookvale Primary School, Erdington

Invisibility Girl

As brave as a lion,
As sneaky as a tiger,
As rapid as a cheetah,
As quiet as a mouse,
As smart as a bookworm,
Masked from the villains,
Hero of the citizens,
Solving problems day and night,
Working like a superstar,
As transparent as glass,
Leaving no shadow behind,
She is Invisibility Girl.

Asiya Hannah Khan (8)
Brookvale Primary School, Erdington

My Astral Projection

I can be in space
Have a gaze
And blaze around

Look at the constellations
Full of imaginations
Dancing with animations

My astral projection
Can't have dejection
It has a connection

With the stars
All in a jar.

Warren Y (10)
Brookvale Primary School, Erdington

Diamonds On The Moon

An astronaut goes in the rocket
He lands on the moon
When he lands on the moon
He starts digging
He finds some diamonds
When he got back to Earth
He lost the diamonds
And he was shocked.

Aarav Verma (7)
Brookvale Primary School, Erdington

My Life (Teenage Me)

I can never be the one for anyone,
I can never find the one,
What is the one?
The one that loves you unconditionally,
The one that sacrifices everything for you,
The one that would fight for you,
Do anything to protect you,
Do they exist out there?
Will they ever exist out there?
Do they only exist in my imagination?
My imagination that's filled with rainbows and butterflies,
Allies,
Everyone tells me,
Love is pain,
Love hurts again and again,
Love is hard to explain,
But it's also hard to obtain,
It's hard like a mountain,
It's hard to contain,
Yet I still search for it,
I still want to be missed,
Knowing he doesn't exist,

It's hard to find those out there,
It's hard in real life.

Vanessa Solyga (9)
Harris Academy Tottenham, London

Hiking In Epping Forest With My Friends

As the shining, glistening sun rose up into the expansive blue sky,
I saw white, majestic birds, flapping their wings way up high.
Looking from side to side, all I could see was more green, lush trees.
Going from bush to bush and collecting lots of succulent, big blackberries,

Spending time with friends and family is precious,
Even though my brother is very annoying and ferocious.

All you have to know is to be happy for what you have,
And don't ask for more,
And make sure to explore!

Maryam Harrou (9)
Harris Academy Tottenham, London

Eco Environment Code

E co club is fun
N ever waste electricity, since it's a waste
V ery small litter makes our environment dirty
I nstead of wasting food, put it in the compost
R eduse, reuse, recycle, three Rs
O nly take things you need
N ature is beautiful, so make it clean
M ore plants, more energy
E nergy gives you breath
N o electricity needed. This is the best so live the rest
T reat our environment like you would like to be treated.

Timilehin Olusomoka (9)
Harris Academy Tottenham, London

You Will Always Be My Friend

You were my best friend. We shared every tear
And felt each other's fear.
You listened to all that I said and never complained.
You truly understood me and always knew what to say.
But, somewhere along the road, we drifted miles apart.
It broke my heart and made me cry,
Suddenly we were different people with nothing the same,
But neither of us could be blamed.
It was like having a lock without its key.

Farida Mostafa (9)
Harris Academy Tottenham, London

Space

Space, a wonderful place
Stars will prance with grace
Space, still a wonderful place

Sky as pink as roses
Clouds as white as cotton
Space is a wonderful place

Rockets dashing in the sky
Get a helmet or you die
Just please try

Space, a wonderful place
Stars will prance with grace
Space will always be a wonderful place.

Naylaa Shaik (9)
Harris Academy Tottenham, London

Guess My Season

I am a season
When leaves have fallen
And trees have frozen.
I'm really cold,
And my days are short.
In this season, trees are hung up
And decorated with shining ornaments.
Animals are hiding,
Waiting for the heat
And their treats
Are already eaten.
During this season, it's meant to snow
And that's a clue for you to know.

Abby Toska (9)
Harris Academy Tottenham, London

Fabulous Felines

F luffy
E legant
L oveable
I ntelligent
N aughty
E ntertaining
S leepy.

Jude Royles (10)
Harris Academy Tottenham, London

All The Seasons

There are four seasons all together,
Some warm and some cold,
They're not all the same weather,
Winter, autumn, summer, spring.

Autumn is when the leaves fall,
It makes a big pile of them,
Some piles are short or tall,
Winter, autumn, summer, spring.

Winter is when it is cold,
You can play with snow,
Some Christmas stories can be told,
Winter, autumn, summer, spring.

Spring is when it gets warmer,
Flowers start to grow,
You can maybe hear farmers,
Winter, autumn, summer, spring.

Summer is really hot,
You can wear sun hats, shorts and T-shirts,
People buy ice lollies and ice cream a lot,
Winter, autumn, summer, spring.

Harriet Thomas (9)
Houghton-On-The-Hill Church Of England Primary School,
Houghton On The Hill

Grandpa's Old Speech

Back in my day
My grandpa used to say
Back in my day
It wasn't quite the same
There weren't any consoles
For us to play our games
We used chalkboards
In our class
For us to write our maths
We played outside in the light
Until it was the night
I know, I know, I replied
Now what's the big deal
He would say
People now don't respect the trees,
The air, the field
You need to learn to respect the world,
'Cause that's how it is
You need to learn to kiss the world,
Hug it how it is.

Penelope Cadman (9)
Houghton-On-The-Hill Church Of England Primary School,
Houghton On The Hill

A Message From The Earth

I am the Earth,
The Earth I am,
I watch over my beauty,
But cry in some lands.

Even though I'm big,
Even though I'm tough,
You still need to care,
As I provide you with much.

Over my fields,
Over my seas,
You can feel the magic,
Where friendships meet.

To the shining stars,
To the bottom of the ocean,
People hurt me,
As they cause commotion.

If you don't take care of me,
Who knows?
As I am a gift,
Which should forever glow.

Pavan Manak (9)
Houghton-On-The-Hill Church Of England Primary School,
Houghton On The Hill

A Journey Through History

Bang, and it began.
Over time matter formed.
It got hot quickly.

Planets and stars came.
Earth was dry without blue water.
Rain fell heavily.

Now life could begin.
In the sea, weird strange things moved.
Volcanic soup food.

Weird snails, ugly crabs.
The Cambrian explosion.
Next up dinosaurs.

Boom, now they are gone.
Oh, hey, here come the mammals.
The start of humans.

Poppy Line (9)
Houghton-On-The-Hill Church Of England Primary School, Houghton On The Hill

Halloween!

H aunting horror throughout the night.
A ll is quiet, then there's a fright!
L aughing children, trick or treating,
L ooking for sweets that they can be eating.
O *ooooow!*
W itches, goblins, ghouls and ghosts,
E very one of them wanting to scare you the most!
E vil, eerie, enchanted times.
N eed we be scared or is this just a rhyme?

Eemia Popat (9)
Houghton-On-The-Hill Church Of England Primary School,
Houghton On The Hill

Heartful

Emeralds green,
Rubies red,
There's no such thing as a stupid head.

Everyone has minds in different guises,
From tiny ant brains to blue whales' huge sizes.

People can say that they're super smart,
But that's because they know you're way past the start.

Now nobody is perfect or yet has brains so big,
But everyone has a heart way bigger than a fig.

Faye Kingham (10)
Houghton-On-The-Hill Church Of England Primary School, Houghton On The Hill

My Seasonal Experiences Of 2024

It was the lovely spring and the beautiful flowers were blooming
I saw a fox
At first I was scared but then my mum told me that the fox was not going to do any harm
I liked the sight of my little foxy friend.

It was the hot summer and the animals scattered around the field
After I finished looking up at the green leaves
I looked down and saw a roe with its family
The little roe walked in the long grass
It felt good when it felt safe around me and didn't run away.

It was the yellow, orange and red autumn
When I walked around the park I stumbled across a red squirrel
That was collecting acorns for the winter
It was a very busy squirrel going up and down the trees
To hide its food safely
I wouldn't like to be a squirrel
It is a busy thing to be.

It was the coldest month of the year
I took a December trip to the zoo
And saw a polar bear
He was sad and alone without any friends.

Julia Ratajczak (9)
Norwich Road Academy, Thetford

Make The World Green

Lives are crying because it's not clean,
Earth is dying because it's not green.

Earth is our dear mother. Don't pollute it,
She gives us food and shelter. Just salute it.

With global warming, it's in danger,
Let's save it by becoming a strong ranger.

With dying trees and animals, it's in sorrow,
Make her green today and green tomorrow.

With melting snow, one day it will sink,
How can we save it? Just think.

Trees are precious. Preserve them,
Water is treasure. Reserve it.

Grow more trees. Make Mother Earth green,
Reduce pollution and make her a queen.

Manna Santhosh (9)
Norwich Road Academy, Thetford

This Is How Life Is

There is a time in life when you get whatever you want,
But that time vanishes in the blink of an eye,
You get more mature,
You stress about your studies,
You have family problems
You go through puberty,
And, as you grow up like this,
You won't even have time to think back
To what a happy life you had as a kid,
But don't let that stop you from trying,
You will go through a lot of pain,
But that pain is a path to your success.

Afrin Aara (10)
Norwich Road Academy, Thetford

I Wish I Was A Leopard

I wish I was a leopard
So spotty, hiding in the trees
I could run as fast as a train
I could catch everything I see

I wish I was a leopard
So I could roar as loud as thunder
I would scare the little creatures
They would all hide down under

I wish I was a leopard
I would be so fierce and scary
Everyone would fear me
But I'm really soft and furry

I wish I was a leopard
Because they are so cool.

Ariella Wood (10)
Norwich Road Academy, Thetford

Feelings

Things that make me sad,
A gloomy, rainy day.
Birthdays, gifts, songs and dancing,
Cheer me up.

Things that make me mad,
People who break promises.
People who lie and when,
Life isn't fair.

Things that make me calm,
A smile from a friend.
Singing and dancing.

Things that make me happy,
Friends,
Family,
Singing and dancing.
And a nice poem to end it all.

Samantha Tucker (10)
Norwich Road Academy, Thetford

The Hero

There once was a man,
Unknown to the crowd,
Never acting for praise,
Not for money,
So here's to the ones,
Who fight without fame,
He stood tall in silence,
While others would sleep,
The hero I know,
The man I adore,
He's been my guide, my heart,
I am with a hero,
That much is true,
And that hero, Dad, is you.

Vihaan Tirumalasetty (10)
Norwich Road Academy, Thetford

My Silly Guinea Pigs

Monday's guinea pig loves to chew
Tuesday's guinea pig is looking at you
Wednesday's guinea pig is always sleepy
Thursday's guinea pig is chewing grass
Friday's guinea pig is gnawing sticks
Saturday's guinea pig is looking at his food
And Sunday's guinea pig will play today.

Teja Zinkeviciute (10)
Norwich Road Academy, Thetford

The Ghost That Worked In The Mill

There was a house on a hill.
With a ghost named Bill.
Who used to work in the mill.
Bill became best friends with Gill.
Gill worked in the mill.
Bill gave a pickle to Gill.

Penelope Ffitch (10)
Norwich Road Academy, Thetford

Stars Beyond The Sky

In the darkness, stars appear,
Sparkling wishes, bright and clear.
Galaxies swirl, and comets glide,
Come explore this cosmic ride!

Mars is red, with dusty plains,
Jupiter's storms dance like wild trains.
Saturn's rings twirl, shiny and round,
In this space playground, joy is found.

So grab your rocket, let's blast off fast,
Through twinkling stars, we'll zoom and blast.
With space as our playground, let's laugh and cheer,
Exploring new worlds, with nothing to fear!

We'll meet friendly aliens, wave hello,
Share our stories, watch their smiles grow.
Together we'll dance on the rings of Saturn,
In this cosmic adventure, there's always a pattern.

So when the sky falls and you look above,
Remember the wonders, the magic, the love.
For in the vast sky, dreams can take flight,
In the heart of the universe, everything's bright.

Saxon Edwards (9)
Outwoods Edge Primary School, Loughborough

Snow White's Death

On the top of a hill,
In a fantasy world,
Lived an adventurous and musical
Gullible girl.

She loved to sing,
To all the birds,
And soon they'd join in too,
Whistling the words.

But far, far away,
A nasty witch resided,
She was very cruel,
Blackhearted and evil-minded.

She wanted to be the prettiest,
Best-looking girl at the ball,
But that was impossible,
As Snow White was the fairest of them all.

The witch didn't like it,
And so she hatched a bad, evil plan,
To poison Snow White,
And wipe her from the world of man.

And off she went,
To the young girl's home,
And planted a poisonous apple,
And away she went, the ruthless old crooked crone.

Snow White looked towards her fruit bowl,
The poisoned apple glistened and gleamed,
Her thoughts wandered and her tummy rumbled,
The apple was not what she had deemed.

She wondered and pondered,
Till she couldn't take it any more,
Snow White took a bite,
And dropped to the floor.

Her complexion even fairer,
She took her last breath,
Her eyes closed shut,
Falling to a sleepy death.

Anaiya Noghan (10)
Outwoods Edge Primary School, Loughborough

Hooray It's Autumn!

In autumn,
Leaves go black, red, yellow and orange.
Crunchy leaves in really big piles.
After autumn it's winter,
But not yet because it's autumn,
Hooray!
You've just had summer when it's hot,
You're meant to wear suncream all day!
In autumn it's Halloween,
Spooooooooooky but also fun.
In autumn it's Bonfire Night,
When it was the gunpowder plot,
Pumpkins start to grow,
And leaves fall off trees.
You have to start to wear your warm trackie bottoms and long-sleeved jumpers.
Autumn is one season before winter,
When Father Christmas comes and gives you lots of presents.
When it's Halloween,
You go trick or treating in costumes.
I love autumn because of the leaves on the ground,
In big, huge, ginormous piles,
Do you like autumn?

Lily Brennan (7)
Outwoods Edge Primary School, Loughborough

My Day

My day goes fast, with a little bit of grunting,
Walking and running, whilst I'm hunting,
With lots of green, vine-like bunting,
While I watch humans, gracefully punting,
And I listen to the heavy drip-drops of the rain,
I stumble as the creature I've caught moans in pain,
The thunder roars, after flashes of bright lightning,
Oh, how so very frightening,
As loud booms are sounding,
Leaves overhead are crashing,
Their branches lashing,
Everything is going wild,
Now, nothing is mild,
I curl up in my lair,
As silent as a hare,
Lots of the animals feel homeless and scared,
But I feel happy and safe and cared.

Jaguar

Amy D'Oyly-Watkins (8)
Outwoods Edge Primary School, Loughborough

Football Fun

We arrive at the football pitch, all excited
We join up with our teammates and we are all united
We warm up and discuss tactics
Our family and friends start to arrive
And they are all fanatics
We step up onto the football pitch all happy and excited
Not knowing what's going to happen.
Then the ref blows the whistle to start
And everyone plays their part
And when you finally get the ball
You dribble and kick.
And when you score you will shout hooray!
Because you have done your achievement of the day
Football is here for fun and laughter
So we keep playing forever after!

Freya Butler (10)
Outwoods Edge Primary School, Loughborough

Dog Breeds

Short hair or long hair
Skinny or round
There are lots of dog breeds that are around
The poodle, intelligent and loyal
With a coat so curly
But be aware, they like to wake up early!
Then there's the dachshund
Also known as the sausage dog
Small in size but with adorable eyes
They like to bark
But also walk in the park
They will win your heart!
The German shepherd
A bigger breed
Will help you if you are in need
They will come when you call
And even bring you a ball
Dogs are the best. They are my favourite
As you can guess!

Sienna Musson (9)
Outwoods Edge Primary School, Loughborough

A Magical Day!

Once, a girl was under a tree,
Whilst drinking a cup of tea,
Her favourite thing to do was read,
Could she read?
She could indeed,
Then, a rabbit hopped along,
The very first glare was way too long,
Then, the girl went on her knees,
Welcoming the rabbit with a piece of cheese,
Then, it scurried behind the girl,
Doing so with a bit of a twirl,
After a bit,
Where I sit,
Became illegal,
To a golden eagle,
I had drunk too much dairy,
Then I saw a beautiful fairy,
She was my friend,
And, that's the end.

Lyla Walker (9)
Outwoods Edge Primary School, Loughborough

Friendship Never Ends

A friend is someone who makes me smile
We laugh and play for a long long while.
They share their toys and know what's right,
They help me out when things feel tight.

We run around and have some fun,
We talk and play until we're done.
In good times, bad times, day or night,
A friend makes everything feel bright.

When I'm sad they sit with me,
We dream of places we want to see
Giggling and laughing, happy with glee.

No matter what, through thick and thin,
Friendship never ends -
It always wins.

Aleena Sudhan (8)
Outwoods Edge Primary School, Loughborough

Dreams Up Above...

Up above in the sky
Down on the floor where you lie
Trying to solve riddles
Then after that you give a giggle
Look over there and you'll see some nature
If you look closer you'll see a creature
Next to some treasure!
When you go to space
Have fun and race
You're in last place
So keep up the pace
In your dreams you'd have fun
And soon you'll wake up and it'll be done
You felt good and joyful
So breathe in and do it slowly and after you can laugh cheerfully!

Ryan Midzi (8)
Outwoods Edge Primary School, Loughborough

Four Mini Seasons

Spring, to me, feels like a breeze,
As it flows by,
Flowers on my face,
They don't make me cry.

In the summer,
The rays on my face,
Sat on a sun lounge,
As I hear splashes of the sea.

Now in autumn,
Big and strong,
All the trees are yellow and strong,
I crunch the leaves under my feet,
Very cool and very neat.

Winter is the last season,
And this is the reason
That this is the most fun season,
As it's when the snow comes.

Thomas Porter (8)
Outwoods Edge Primary School, Loughborough

Space

I saw an alien up in space, floating in an endless race.
There are nine planets up in space;
They cannot scare me with their empty grace.
Between stars upon starts where no human races,
Space is a place of wonder, with no thunder.

On the moon, you won't find a baboon.
The air is frozen, there is no light,
And the vastness is overwhelming, incredible and bright.
I carry within me, much nearer home,
The power to scare myself with my own desert places.

Zlata Dimitrova (10)
Outwoods Edge Primary School, Loughborough

My Dog, Coco

You were my best friend.
Always there for me when I was sad,
You gave me lots of love and cuddles.
When my day was really bad.

You liked to play my games with me.
And made me happy when I was alone.
We made lots of lovely memories.
And took selfies together on my phone.

I miss you every single day.
I wish we had more time to play.
And I know you are happy above the clouds.
Where you can run, jump and play all day.

Courtney-Leigh Holland (9)
Outwoods Edge Primary School, Loughborough

Out In Nature

Trees are tall, they touch the sky,
The birds all sing and fly.
The grass is green,
The clouds drift by,
They're oh so soft.

The river flows with a gentle sound,
It's never bound.
The flowers bloom colours bright,
They dance in the wind, they feel just right.

The sun shines down,
It warms my face.
Nature's here, so big and wide,
I love it all, I can't hide.

Loki MacTavish (7)
Outwoods Edge Primary School, Loughborough

Walk

Leaves rustle beneath my feet,
Snowflakes fall on my head,
Puddles splash under my feet,
Birds fly above my head, tweeting at each other,
Sticks snap as I step on them,
A squirrel runs in front of me and squeaks at me,
Deer sip from a running stream in the forest,
Brown, crumbly leaves fall from the surrounding trees,
When I get back home,
I cuddle in a blanket and watch the snow fall.

Sophie Killick (10)
Outwoods Edge Primary School, Loughborough

Sports I Like Doing

Football is my favourite sport
I like to score lots of goals
We play as a team
Being a professional footballer is my dream

I also like basketball
I like shooting shots and scoring
We block people's passes
People watch us in their masses

I like playing cricket
I can bowl and bat
We like getting runs and getting people out
The people scream and shout.

Jaxon Bryans (8)
Outwoods Edge Primary School, Loughborough

Beautiful Beaches

Sun goes bright, sea stays light.
The distance of trees fills my sight.
The thought of peace seems very nice.
As I lay there filled with bliss,
I can smell a candle of swiss
When the sky turns from grey to blue,
On that beach it's only you.
As you thoroughly look at the amazing view,
You will realise beaches are not skewed
But they're *beautiful!*

Tishya Miglani (9)
Outwoods Edge Primary School, Loughborough

Halloween Night

One spooky night,
Costumes are scary,
People are trick or treating,
Knocking on the doors, making scary faces,
Houses are decorated to scare,
Lots of buckets full of treats and sweets,
But, something is different this year,
With more pumpkins in the windows,
Cats with witches' costumes on,
Everybody is happy,
On this spooky night.

Emilie Garvin (7)
Outwoods Edge Primary School, Loughborough

Christmas Eve

Tinsel shines,
Lights glimmer,
Everyone's happy when Christmas comes around,
Presents are under the tree when children are having a good night's sleep,
Santa's up in the sky, waiting for everyone to fall asleep,
Will he come to you?
Have you been naughty this year?
Because you have been peeping at your presents.

Bella Bennion (9)
Outwoods Edge Primary School, Loughborough

Be Nice To Save The Planet

I was walking down the street
When I saw a bird and
Heard it chirp.
It had blue spots and then it stopped.
My dad chucked some rubbish in the bin.
The bird swooped down and
Grabbed the tin.
The bird flew away to its nest
To have a rest.
This could hurt the bird
That's why we save
The planet.

Rory Ward (7)
Outwoods Edge Primary School, Loughborough

Beautiful Seasons

Seasons are different,
Some are warm, some are cold,
But they are all magnificent,
Spring is great for planting,
Summer is great for harvesting,
Everyone starts collecting food for eating,
The same thing with squirrels,
But a little bit different,
They hide acorns,
To eat them in winter.

Petr Borisov (7)
Outwoods Edge Primary School, Loughborough

My Book

My book is my refuge
I go in
To leave the world behind.

It makes me feel calmer
Away from everything
Going to a new world.

Happy, sad, scared or excited
Good or bad
Exploring all of my emotions.

My book is my refuge
I go in
To leave the world behind.

Evie Headley (10)
Outwoods Edge Primary School, Loughborough

Mother

M y mother is amazing.
O ther mums are too.
T ogether they can make people's day.
H onestly it's true.
E ach one is different and has their own super mum powers
R eally the ones that are the best though are the ones that give warm hugs for hours.

Emily Russell (8)
Outwoods Edge Primary School, Loughborough

Dragons

Dragons, their fiery breath,
Their lust for death,
Dragons, their sharp claws,
Their smooth paws,
Dragons, their black eyes,
The way one flies,
Dragons, beautiful and fiery,
I believe they're real,
I hope you do too,
If you do, we can make it come true!

Oscar McGowan (9)
Outwoods Edge Primary School, Loughborough

Sugar!

Sugar is so sweet
It makes me get to my feet
And listen to the beat
Replaying in my head
So I can't ever go to bed
Sugar in any shape or form
Brownies, lollipops, sweets
I want it all
Sweet sugar makes me smile
I'm gonna be hyper all the while.

Sienna Hall (9)
Outwoods Edge Primary School, Loughborough

Space Like You've Never Known It

As we get into our rockets, we fly so high,
I see Mars and Jupiter getting close,
Then, I see Saturn,
I jump on its rings,
As I skate around the rings of Saturn,
I remember something;
I need to get back to my rocket, to Earth,
And home is where I'll be.

Amelia Smith (8)
Outwoods Edge Primary School, Loughborough

Autumn Leaves

Autumn leaves come down from trees of fire,
Colours fall down, spirits rise higher,
People sing, accompanied by gusts of wind
Say farewell to the sun, Halloween, here we come!
Honey tea warms you to the core,
One plump pumpkin, come on, we want more!

Imogen Lane (9)
Outwoods Edge Primary School, Loughborough

Falling

A haiku

Leaves descend from high,
Silently fluttering down,
Between life and death.

Louis Dale (7)
Outwoods Edge Primary School, Loughborough

Henry VIII's Wives

H enry should've died
E ven some survived
N ext, someone died
R eally, three died
Y es, I'm really horrified.

Jamie Hicks (8)
Outwoods Edge Primary School, Loughborough

Friends

Friends are very important
Because they are not just for playing with,
They're also there for helping you
When you are sad, worried or even hurt.

Esme Maden (9)
Outwoods Edge Primary School, Loughborough

Nightfall

A haiku

The ravenous dark,
Swallows radiant sunshine,
Bleak night is coming.

Violet Dale (10)
Outwoods Edge Primary School, Loughborough

Maths

M aths,
A lso known as mathematics,
T hough it can be
H ard, you try your best,
S o, reach for the stars.

Adam Howe (9)
Outwoods Edge Primary School, Loughborough

Chocolate Universe

Chocolates from the galaxy
Chocolates galore
Chocolates in your pockets
To place upon your paw.

Beth Gardner (8)
Outwoods Edge Primary School, Loughborough

Bees Flying

Bees fly everywhere,
With a buzz and a zoom,

They fly here, to the roses,
They fly there, to the clover bloom,

Collecting golden pollen,
Dusting their fuzzy knees,

Everywhere they fly,
A gentle, humming breeze.

They make noise,
A busy, buzzy sound,
Everywhere,
The bees fly all around.

Chisom Chinedu (7)
Pelham Primary School, London

Friendship

Friendship is *love* and *happiness*

Friendship is a fragile budding *flower* in spring

Friendship is the soft *touch* of your pet when you are sad

Friendship is a *lighthouse* in a fierce storm

Friendship is a *tornado* that knocks you off your feet

Friendship is a favourite *ice cream* on a hot, sunny day

Friendship is the *warmth* of spitting sparks of the fire

Friendship is the *smell* of hot chocolate after a long walk

Friendship is the *miracle* of Christmas

Friendship is your *mum's* cuddle before going to sleep

Friendship is for *everyone*!

Sofiia Khoteeva (7)
Pelham Primary School, London

Arya And Sansa's Journey

Arya and Sansa started their journey,
It took them a ten-hour flight,
They landed upon the great Amazon,
With a loud bang and crash,
The plane made a big splash,
As it crashed into the crocodile's lair,
The crocodiles started chomping pieces of the plane,
Arya and Sansa scampered away,
Next they found snakes slithering in the trees,
"Ssss, you better watch out,"
As Arya and Sansa scampered away,
They finally made it out of the Amazon,
By carving tools made out of trees to fix the plane,
What a journey this has been for Arya and Sansa.

Brody Watson (9)
Pelham Primary School, London

The Taylor Swift Poem Of Songs

T aylor Swift now has
A Place In This World for her music
Y ou're Not Sorry after you listen to one of her songs
L ong Live her reputation
O nly The Young Taylor is listened to
R un straight to her concert

S afe And Sound is how you feel when you hear one of her songs
"W elcome To New York!" her fans scream as she arrives for her tour
I Can See You listening to her songs
F orever And Always
T he Best Days are always when I listen to one of her songs.

Evie Johnson (9)
Pelham Primary School, London

The Zoo

Haiku poetry

I went to the zoo
I laughed at the giraffe poo!
My friends giggled too

I saw a fruit bat
The gorillas were quite fat
Monkeys like to chat.

Loved the lion's den
The goats played in a brown pen
I'd visit again.

Xavier Phillip-Andrew (8)
Pelham Primary School, London

Rainforest

R ainy days, day after day
A xolotls swimming in the lake
I guanas crawling in the mud
N ests all scattered with eggs
F oxes looking for their next prey
O lympic jaguars wanting to win the next prey competition.
R ainforests filled with mud as the waterfall goes dripping down.
E asy peasy alligators are against the jaguar because he wants to win.
S nakes slithering across rocks and strangled vines
T igers yelling out big roars to get other people's attention.

Marwa Khan (8)
Pelham Primary School, London

Rainforests

Lush trees,
Clean air,
The creatures that live here are happy.

But these days, trees cry,
They say they are sick,
As people constantly cut and cut their ankles with axes.

Animals also cry,
They say they are scared,
As their houses keep getting cut down and they are being made homeless.

I also cry,
I'm so afraid,
As I won't have enough air to breathe.

All the creatures that live on the planet will cry,
Please stop cutting the trees!
Please stop!

Sunu Park (8)
Pelham Primary School, London

Halloween

H orrifying masks sprinting down the road,
A ll Hallows' Eve, everyone's gone rogue!
L ollies and treats next to carved pumpkin faces,
L ots of children running door-to-door races,
O ut in the dark on a starry autumn night,
W itches and wizards giving us a fright,
E veryone's knocking to get their treats,
E ach spooky bucket overflowing with lots and lots of sweets!
N aughty children shouting, "Trick or treat!"

Cassia Reed (9)
Pelham Primary School, London

My Light

Where is the light?
It's lighting up my toilet.

Where is the light?
It's lighting up the living room where my family talk harmoniously.

Where is the light?
It's lighting up my family table of delicious food.

Where is the light?
It's lighting up my room,
When it's dark, I'm not scared, because there's light.

Even in the night sky,
The twinkle star is shining.

Dayeon Lee (7)
Pelham Primary School, London

One Day I Went To The Supermarket

One day I went to the supermarket,
I saw some chicken breast,
But I really was not impressed,
So I went to the veggie aisle,
To get some peas,
But I looked over,
And saw some mini trees,
I was just a kid,
So I put one in my mouth,
And that was when my shopping trip went south,
Because broccoli is disgusting,
When you are small,
I do not like broccoli,
I don't like it at all!

Penelope Buchanan (7)
Pelham Primary School, London

Autumn Wind

A utumn wind is blowing
U mbrellas go inside out
T owering trees with a gentle breeze
U nderneath lie golden leaves
M isty fog fills the air
N aughty squirrels steal nuts

W hen it rains go inside
I nsects scuttle along the ground
N o more sun, a blast of wind
D arkness steals the evening light.

Ether Cobblah (9)
Pelham Primary School, London

The Mouse House

I changed my house with a mouse
I crossed the road with a mouse and a house
But there is a house with a mouse
And a cat, meow meow
And it ate me up, yum yum
But there was another mouse getting eaten, by a *cat!*
Over there is a mouse, a cat, also a house
What a wonderful dream they will have next
But they could make friends with a bat wearing a hat.

Ayda Byrne (7)
Pelham Primary School, London

Away The Forest Goes

The forest goes away
Every time I take a step in the city.
Floppy, I go home
Dreaming of singing with birds,
Dancing with squirrels
And walking with snails.
At home, I wonder
What would happen the next day...
Went to the forest to find peace
And found the most beautiful bird in the world.
It had deer horns and it was all blue.
I loved it!

Sofia Rigoli (7)
Pelham Primary School, London

Mummy

Mummy is as graceful as a swan.
Unconditional love all around.
Beautiful always inside and out.
She makes yummy meals just for me.

Mummy's hugs are huge, warm and wide.
With magical moments by her side.
Mummy helps with homework and looks after me.
With love, kindness and pride.
Mummy loves me no matter what.
And I love her too.

Matilda Packwood (7)
Pelham Primary School, London

Ode To My Teacher

She's nice, she's lovely, she's awfully kind,
Every day she nurtures our mind,
All different things to do every day,
She teaches us subjects in lots of new ways,
She's very helpful, buzzing with care,
With luscious and long, nice bouncy hair,
If we need answers, she'll make us look,
Most of the time, we find answers in a book.

Olivia Mannion (9)
Pelham Primary School, London

Rainbows And Wildlife

Rainbows shining around beautifully across the world.
Colours shimmer so bright.
The sun shines bright, its gentle light helps flowers blossom.
The birds sing happily.
The butterflies flap their wings in the sky.
Raindrops fall on the grass and make beautiful plants and flowers.
Remember, enjoy the rainbows and wildlife.

Sara Nandagopal (8)
Pelham Primary School, London

Positive Words

P retty
E xcellent
L ove
H appy
A mazing
M ulti-school

P erfect
O ptimistic
E xciting
M agical

M ariam
A mazing
R emember
I nteresting
A wesome
M arvellous.

Mariam Choudhury (7)
Pelham Primary School, London

Pandas

P andas eating bamboo all day long.
A ll the time when they have babies, they feed when they're hungry.
N ot every single panda can have a baby.
D eep in the forest, pandas are sleeping all day long.
A lso, pandas can get tired when they're looking after their baby pandas.

Safa Khan (7)
Pelham Primary School, London

Magic

M agic will always help you if you learn how to use it well.
A mazing things can happen if you know fantastic spells.
G reat things will happen if you practise your magic skills.
I magination is incredible like magic.
C an you use your own imagination to create your own magic?

Lía Sánchez Conesa (7)
Pelham Primary School, London

Music

Music is so calm sometimes
Yet so intensifying other times
With the piano and violin
Classical is everything
The drums and guitar are so cool
They make you want to move!
All music is fun
So have a party under the sun
With the beats going on
You'll love this song!

Harper Gregorowski (8)
Pelham Primary School, London

Glass Frogs

Glistening in the warm sunlight,
They jump through the bright, green leaves,
Waking all the others,
Once they are all awake,
The forest hums with noise,
Through the gap between the leaves,
You will discover a forest waiting to be seen.

Bethany Bartlett (8)
Pelham Primary School, London

Stars

Stars, stars, beautiful stars
You live up high in the sky and
Only shine at night
Oh... if I can touch them, I hope
I can grab ten
Stars, stars, beautiful stars
I will put you in a big jar
Where all my dreams will come true.

Manuel Tranquilli (7)
Pelham Primary School, London

Friends

F orgive you if you have an argument
R espect you in everything
I nclude you in games
E ncourage you at new things
N eed you
D eserve you
S ave you if something goes wrong.

Giorgia Davis (9)
Pelham Primary School, London

A Wonderful Rainy Day

Some people don't like the rain, some people do,
I like the rain when I'm with you,
Happy trees and happy flowers, they all love their little showers,
So say hooray to the rain,
And I hope to see it soon again.

Alice Berry (9)
Pelham Primary School, London

Kids

Kids have to study,
And learn,
Every day.

Kids have to play,
And enjoy,
Their day.

Kids need to eat,
And to sleep.

Kids need a family,
Who gives love,
And care.

Tomas Ferreira Fernandes (7)
Pelham Primary School, London

Our Wonderful World

A haiku

Through the tangled vines
Rainbow toucans and birds fly
This is paradise.

Avi Daren (8)
Pelham Primary School, London

The Mouse Who Changed House

There once was a mouse
Who lived in a house
He once met a louse
The mouse changed house
And there he met a grouse
He again changed house.

Alice Aldridge (7)
Pelham Primary School, London

Day And Night

Diamante Poem

Sun
Bright, shiny
Melting, illuminating, waking
Sunglasses, fire, rock, mooncake
Relaxing, sleeping, smiling
Shy, mysterious
Moon.

Giselle So (8)
Pelham Primary School, London

Best Teacher

M agical
I mportant
S uper
S mart

T all
U nderstanding
C aring
K ind.

Clemmie Cullen (9)
Pelham Primary School, London

Animals Of The Rainforest

A haiku

Glass frog camouflaged
Venomous snake slithering
Jaguar preying.

Emily Wolman (8)
Pelham Primary School, London

Snakes Killing

A haiku

A slither slither
Unpredictable, deadly
Constrictors killing.

Henry Barnes (8)
Pelham Primary School, London

Cosy Season

Autumn is coming
Leaves are falling
The air is cold
Hot chocolate and marshmallows
Fold your scarves
Let's go outside.

Kiara Nandagopal (8)
Pelham Primary School, London

Tubes

T wisting tunnels
U nderground tubes
B usy escalators
E xciting journeys.

Fred Paton (7)
Pelham Primary School, London

Untitled

W inter is the time when it's white and snowy
I n winter you need to wear a scarf, gloves and a hat
N ot a tank top and shorts, no, no, no
T en weeks later it's Christmas, when Santa comes
E veryone at Christmas thinks about Jesus and spending time with family
R ight below the stars, the white soft snow falls

A t Christmas in winter opening presents
T ime has come, yay, yay, yay

C hristmas has come, time to open presents
H appy times are the best, like Christmas
R ight in the sky is sparkling, shining stars are twinkling
I n the sky
S o time has come, let's celebrate
T ime has come, let's open presents and see the Christmas lights
M any people celebrate, but not some
A nd we go to bed late but too late and Santa won't come
S un comes out but it still won't be hot like summer, and still be cold.

Ellie Jones (9)
Saxon Way Primary School, Gillingham

Christmas Day

Once upon a Christmas, in a faraway house,
Arose such a clatter, what else?
All their stockings hung on their beds,
Snug and Tug sleeping the night away,
For it was Christmas Day.

Waiting for morning to open presents,
What will they get? A dog? Who knows?
For Christmas is here, of course it is.
Deep in their sleep,
They dream about gingerbread and Christmas feasts,
Swirling around in their heads.

Santa is checking his list twice,
To see if they are naughty or nice.
For this is Christmas, Christmas indeed.

As Santa flies in his wonderful sleigh,
Reindeers of magic, sing away.
Each house is filled with joy waiting for Christmas Day.
For this is Christmas, Christmas indeed.

Hearing carols, singing sweet songs, raising money for charity.

Oh no, it's Mr Scrooge, what will we do?
Christmas is over, over indeed.
Or is it?

Olivia Mclaren (9)
Saxon Way Primary School, Gillingham

Wishes We All Want

If I were a genie, I would grant the wishes of:
To be faster than the flashy Flash,
To be stronger than Mike Tyson (when he was young)
To be as intelligent as William James Sidis,
To be a polyglot, to know many languages like Spanish, German.

If I were a genie, I would grant the wishes of:
To be better than C Ronaldo and Messi at football,
To be better than Michael Phelps at swimming,
To be better than Michael Jordan, Steph Curry and LeBron James (Kobe).

If I were to be a genie, I would grant the wishes of:
To be the CEO of Apple and Samsung,
To be the CEO of Amazon and social media,
To have my own successful business.

If I were to be a genie, I would grant the wishes of:
To be able to talk to animals,
To have a pink and orange night sky (sunset also),
To control the elements of water, fire, lightning, wind and earth.

Dylan Sterling (10)
Saxon Way Primary School, Gillingham

Space Town

One day I land up nowhere
Well somewhere
High in space and far from Earth.
Many people (more like aliens) talking random words,
Oh, I wish I could understand.
Drinking tea but not looking at the sea.
Running like a mouse into their house.
I don't know why, but this tells me why.
There are galaxy fire-breathing dragons.
A dragon stole a baby alien from the ground.
I started to fly and chase the fearsome dragon.
After a spoonful of chasing or even racing,
I got the baby and returned her to her alien mother.
Every one of those aliens clapped for me as I was their hero.
Did you know the dragon was going to cook the baby?!

A riddle: my name starts with one A and also ends with one A.
Who am I?
...Aleeza!

Aleeza Nouman (9)
Saxon Way Primary School, Gillingham

Untitled

M y career is the best in the world
E migrated at seven years old to Barcelona
S hooting in top bins is the best
S coring in football might be hard
I 'm the best footballer in the world.

I 'm the best footballer in Argentina
S hould Messi get paid 11 billion?

T he best goal is by Messi from five yards
H e won three World Cups in six years
E ating healthy is so good.

B est goal from him, from me is 6 yards
E ating Lays crisps, they are the best
S pring gives me a tingle
T ouching trophies is so good.

Ollie Gaydon
Saxon Way Primary School, Gillingham

Upside-Down Earth

I awoke,
My eyes struggled to stay open,
Repeated yawns,
Long eye rubbing,
I went to open the curtains,
My jaw fell,
Like it slipped over a banana,
I stretched my eyes open,
Was I seeing right?

The sky was a ruby red,
My heart felt dizzy,
The sparkling sun was an emerald green,
I had to rub my eyes again,
The grass was an eye-blinding magenta,
I had to pinch myself.

I woke up to shaking,
My mother was there,
I realised it was a dream and my heart thumped in relief,
I am glad it's over, peace.

Esther Akinyemi (10)
Saxon Way Primary School, Gillingham

Hide-And-Seek

Behind the trees, beneath the stairs,
We disappeared in childhood prayers.
Hoping no one would find us soon,
Beneath the watch of the afternoon.

With breaths held tight, we'd close our eyes,
The world turned into sweet disguise.
The seeker's steps would echo near,
Yet all we knew was thrilling fear.

But oh! The joy when we were found,
A squeal of laughter, safe and sound.
In simple games, in quiet peeks,
We lived a thousand hide-and-seeks!

Shambhavi Gupta (10)
Saxon Way Primary School, Gillingham

Emotions

E verybody has emotions.
M ost people are happy and others have bad emotions.
O nly if you tell people your bad emotions, it might feel better.
T o you it might be unknown, but just spit the word out.
I t is only you, a friend, or an adult that can solve it.
O nly if you calm down and tell someone I am sure it will be fine.
N o one can read minds if something is wrong.
S o just be as amazing as you are.

Kameelah Oladipupo (9)
Saxon Way Primary School, Gillingham

Autumn's Delight

A utumn feels like magic all around; crunchy leaves make a sound.
U p in the trees, leaves go red, orange and gold; the season is chilly and quite cold.
T rees swaying left and right. Pumpkins shining through the night.
U nder the trees, leaves will be there wrapping themselves to make a pair.
M uddy leaves here and there while the trees give you a stare.
N arrow trees swinging back and forth. The wind blowing to the north.

Sofia Kennerley (9)
Saxon Way Primary School, Gillingham

Girls 'N' Ghouls

"It's almost Halloween time!"
That's what lots of kids say,
But what they don't know,
Is on Hallows' Eve day,
The ghosts and ghouls
Can start watching you,
You first hear them in the bushes,
Then someone yells, "Boo!"
You may whip your head,
Expecting,
To see a pale-white ghost,
But never mind because you say, "Oh,"
Because you find out that it was,
Your little sister all along!

Sydney Dimond (10)
Saxon Way Primary School, Gillingham

The Supreme Vikings

Long, long ago, across the sea,
Lived powerful warriors bold and free,
With axes and shields so bright they could shine in the night.
They sailed the seven seas from day to night.

Vikings are bold, their hearts dominant and cold.
They'll raid shores of faraway lands and fight
With all their might.

So, I let them cry out to their battles,
The victory is theirs to claim,
As they conquer the Vikings' name!

Iretemide Lawal (10)
Saxon Way Primary School, Gillingham

Fantasy Football

Mythical creatures flying about,
Spiders climbing the water spout,
The grass is green, nice and long,
Birds are singing lovely songs.

In the forest, there was a thump,
Then there was a massive bump,
A small ball, round and clear,
Animals hopping there and here.

The game has started, the crowd cheer,
The goalkeeper is ready, the ball is near,
One, two, three goals are scored,
On the giant scoreboard.

Tekena Clark (9)
Saxon Way Primary School, Gillingham

Nightmare

N ight passed and I went to bed
I have these thoughts that fill my head
G o inside a dark cave
H aving a thought if I would be saved
T he fierce dragon had a lot of fire
M y feet felt like they had taken me higher
A nd then it had opened his mouth
R ealised I was in his snout
E ven when I woke up I was scared.

Tochi Ifeanyi (10)
Saxon Way Primary School, Gillingham

Space And Nature

Space is beautiful
Space is calm
Space is very beautiful, and the galaxy.
When you are in space, there is no air in space.
There are eight planets in the solar system.
The first astronaut in space was Neil Armstrong.

Nature is cool
Nature is amazing
Nature has wonderful things like flowers
And trees
And all of the things on the ground!

Nassir Popoola (9)
Saxon Way Primary School, Gillingham

Untitled

In the mist of the dark,
There is one standing out,
His leadership, bravery, determination and excellence,
Remains to be seen like nobody else,
The football genius Michael Funks,
Michael Funks practises night and day,
There is no stopping him,
Injury after injury,
He stays determined like a tangerine,
This man is a machine, no doubt.

Uwakmfon Nelson (9)
Saxon Way Primary School, Gillingham

Rabbit

R oared the rabbit, so the person could go away, then the rabbit said,
A rabbit is as cute as a cloudy, fluffy
B all,
B ut the rabbit still didn't let the person stroke him,
I like rabbits really badly,
T he carrots look yummy, would you like some? They are really good, I hope you like them, so be a rabbit.

Hannah Stevens (9)
Saxon Way Primary School, Gillingham

Nature Showers

N ature is naturally green.
A utumn is naturally orange with a crunchy sound of gold.
T he birds will chirp until they die with a funny sound of mould.
U ntil it stops the birds will go nowhere but home.
R ocks rumble and tumble when the rocks blow.
E very day and every night the trees will blow with a fright.

Leyton Michael Adams (9)
Saxon Way Primary School, Gillingham

Emotions

E motions can be happy, sad or angry,
M ake your move and have fun,
O n a lovely Tuesday, you may find,
T hat people enjoy themselves,
I n the lovely sun,
O n a glum Friday, many people stay at home,
N ow you know all this,
S tay happy and enjoy being you.

Abdulgaffar Mustrapha (9)
Saxon Way Primary School, Gillingham

The Best Friends

F riends, two BFFs playing.
R iding on a roller coaster.
I n a fair.
E nding the day with a hot cocoa.
N ear the sun. It was the
D ay when they had been to the park.
S nacks and food with their hot cocoa.

Scarlett East (9)
Saxon Way Primary School, Gillingham

The Legend Of The Phoenix

In the dead of night, as dark as the blackest time
Standing in front of me was a grey phoenix
In a blink of my eye, it appeared before me
I expected it to devour me
Instead, it took me for a ride that I will never forget.

Chimebuka Elekwachi (9)
Saxon Way Primary School, Gillingham

Cute Axolotls

Axolotls are as cute as little plushies,
They swim like little fishies,
They are as cute as baby pandas,
Beware of their cuteness as you look in the picture,
You may be shocked as they get older, change happens.

Kitty Collingwood-Taylor (9)
Saxon Way Primary School, Gillingham

The Alternative Nature Universe

The nature creature
Lives in the alternative universe
In a grassy nature place.

Alex
Saxon Way Primary School, Gillingham

The City Of Pompeii 79 AD

The morning started burning hot,
Hotter than a normal day,
As people started the markets,
With the best in Pompeii.

Fresh ripe fruit,
Newly caught fish,
Brand new cloth,
That could make good dish.

A wealthy lady paraded by,
And many people gazed.
She was as pretty as a sunflower,
And looked amazed.

One man looked at Vesuvius,
And told his wife, "Come with me,"
So both of them went through,
And then decided to flee.

He didn't know the panic of 20,000 people in the city,
The falling pumice stones that night,
And all the ash,
You wouldn't want to see the sight,

Everyone rushing about
Like they were late
As fast as cheetahs
They headed for the marine gate

Once they got there
There were no boats
Everyone panicking
And trying to float

Sadly that night
Many people died
And only a handful survived
And the people who died were then multiplied

But today as we dig
We rediscover
The town of Pompeii
Hidden under a cover.

Matilda Simpson (8)
St Thomas More Catholic Voluntary Academy, Leicester

The Great Escape

In the great escape from the zoo
Eight caribou and the gnu they knew
Mounted a minor military coup -
An act of mighty daring do!
And locked the staff they over-threw in the 'pottamus pit and the port-a-loo
Then caught a plane to north Peru

As animals broke out two by two
To squeal and growl and grunt and moo
A loud, unruly queue soon grew
That wriggled, ran, crawled and flew... stampeding down the avenue
While a crocodile and cockatoo crossed the Thames in a stolen canoe
Rowed by the bird so the croc could chew
Through the bones of the eight man crew
'Til the river ran red instead of blue

You doubt my word, what's wrong with you?
Why, every detail here is true
The great escape from the zoo - when was that? I thought you knew
Years ago at half past two!

Elodie Phythian (9)
St Thomas More Catholic Voluntary Academy, Leicester

The Four Super Seasons

The years that we have lived through,
Have four different seasons,
Each is unique for lots of reasons,
In spring, lots of daffodils start to grow,
A fresh, cool breeze will begin to blow,
In summer, it's good to go outside,
Maybe go to the park and go down a slide,
When it fades away, the hot summer tang,
Autumn comes, hear the fireworks bang,
In autumn, it's cool to be very, very keen,
For there are lots of festivals, like Halloween,
In winter, things start to get really jolly,
Decorating your Christmas tree with tinsel and holly,
So the four super seasons are really fun,
Thank you, super seasons, thanks a tonne.

Zahra Hassan (9)
St Thomas More Catholic Voluntary Academy, Leicester

The Big Nature Of Plants, Air And The Grill

On a sunny morning,
The air of nature spread in the world,
Trees grew, making progress, on and on,
Nothing stopped them.

The leaves grew as if nothing was happening,
Leaves as green as vegetables,
The nature knew it was going to be over.

As night came, the grill uncurled itself,
Lifted its hideous head,
And grinned at the city,
As it stomped its way into the road.

As pupils snoozed, the stomp awoke them,
The air force came and he growled,
When the light came on in its eyes, it backed off,
But then, after hours, the city was gone.

Irene Riganello (8)
St Thomas More Catholic Voluntary Academy, Leicester

My First Day On A Pirate Ship

My first day on a pirate ship
Parrots squawked around me
I took a long kip
And from drinking loads of rum
It made me want to pee

My second day on a pirate ship
I walked the plank
A fish gave me a nip
And the captain gave me a spank

My third day on a pirate ship
I found a chest of treasure
Got a scar on my lip
And steered the entire ship
It was a pleasure

My fourth day on a pirate ship
I was really bored
I got a cut from a sword on my hip
And I decided that I didn't want to be on it anymore.

William Addison-Smith (10)
St Thomas More Catholic Voluntary Academy, Leicester

Growing Up

Growing up can be very, very hard,
Which comes with ups and downs,
But no need to have a frown!

Times can be rough,
But you've got to stay tough,
For the world's ecstasy,
Can't you see,
Growing up can be easy peasy!

That means no more diapers,
Cause there is a world waiting for you,
So what's to be waited for, go on,
Open that enchanted door!

No need to ignore!

Because there is a beautiful life to await,
Never have to debate,
You can be free, finally!

Tilly Abbott (8)
St Thomas More Catholic Voluntary Academy, Leicester

Space Vs Race

Two rockets on their first mission,
To find their real position
The wolves looked up to the moon
And soon they started to howl
Two rockets blasted up to space for their first race
They blasted to the moon and they arrived very soon
They went back to Earth and found themselves in the sky so high
The stars were like diamonds
They shone like embers
Howling in deep dark space.

Mayven Gadalla (9)
St Thomas More Catholic Voluntary Academy, Leicester

Song Of The Sky

Up in space, where the stars glow bright.
A shooting star flies right by,
Planets in amazement,
Wishing on the star.
Mercury, Venus,
Earth and Mars.

As the sun says goodbye
And the moon arises
It paints the sky blue and violet.

Kristine Joseph (9)
St Thomas More Catholic Voluntary Academy, Leicester

Fabulous Friends!

There was a girl whose name was Tilly,
She had a friend known as Lilly.
They enjoyed lots of playdates,
And danced together like best mates.

They always achieved their goals together,
And knew they would be friends forever.
They loved to eat sushi and sweets,
And enjoy lots of special treats.

They always had this great connection,
And shared such love and affection.
They had each other to drive away their fears,
And someone beside them to wipe away tears.

Together they were both really silly,
That was the friendship of Tilly and Lilly!

Lottie Foan (9)
St Wilfrid's Catholic Primary School, Angmering

Molly And Mavrick

I have a friend called Molly,
And she is rather jolly,
She has a playful dragon, Mavrick is his name,
They are very alike, they're both insane!

Mavrick is small,
Quite the opposite of tall,
He could fit inside your palm,
He's quite the opposite of calm!

He is so titchy, tiny and blue,
He could fit inside your shoe,
He has powers, water and ice,
And bad habits like eating mice!

The naughty little dragon,
Went outside and saw a weird-looking wagon,
He called Molly,
And she said, "Golly!"

The adventurous pair hopped into the wagon,
Molly first, then the dragon,
It flew them into the air to their shock,
It kept on going, it wouldn't stop!

Until it came to Molly's school,
Then the wagon started to fall,
It landed with a bump on the floor,
Then with a puff, Mavrick opened the door!

As they went in, the whole school saw,
Mavrick gave a friendly roar,
Since that day they laughed with Molly,
Remembering that day so jolly.

Ruth Clarke (9)
St Wilfrid's Catholic Primary School, Angmering

Autumn

A n autumn walk, crackling, shining golden leaves shuffle around on the path.
U p in the trees the chestnut brown conkers nestle in their spiky homes.
T ime for picking pumpkins, orange pops of colour glow in the fields of hardened earth.
U nder bright blue skies, the morning chill makes my cheeks glow in the cold, crisp air.
M y favourite activities in autumn are snuggling under warm fleece blankets with hot chocolate after a cold, colourful walk in the woods.
N ovember brings darker nights with skies lit by fireworks that crackle and bang bright up high.

Daragh MacManus (9)
St Wilfrid's Catholic Primary School, Angmering

The Question Of Existence

There is time everywhere for everyone,
But what is existence?
I'm ambitious to find the answer.
A question of how it exists.
It has been said,
That Earth is efficient,
But now teachers teach everything in school.
They're cool, they rule.
Like everyone thinks about a different religion.
Well, nothing tells us the answer.
Or maybe it does.
We just haven't noticed it...

Well, I say that Earth is just a part of life.
What is there beyond time?
Beyond the solar system,
Beyond the Earth there has to be, right?
We poor humans don't stand a chance,
Of what's out there.
Oh, my dog he brought back the ball, finally.
Poor Snoopy has no idea of what I'm talking about.
Angela.

Angela Passos (9)
Stockwell Primary School, Lambeth

The Spanish Culture

This is Spain and it doesn't really rain,
It has shops and lots of people come.
Spain has food that makes everyone in a good mood.
It's a land that is not bad.
It's the best place in Europe,
And you can chill like a hot chilli.
There are treats,
There are sweets,
And a lot more,
There are funfairs and arcades,
And even soft plays.
There are restaurants to eat at and be able to chill.
Canary Islands are islands of Spain,
Which have canaries and beaches.

Spain has millions of fun things,
So it will be majestic and magical.

People can be rude,
But still, it's a lot better than the United Kingdom.
In the morning, they rise and shine,
And are ready to go.

Dylan Tabares Isaza (7)
Stockwell Primary School, Lambeth

An Adventure Through Time

Millions of years ago
Before the sun could even crawl
Cavemen roamed the earth
And were beautiful

The Egyptians were watching
As the sun was setting
A day's job done
Of building the Pyramids of Giza
Until Alexander the Great conquered

The great Greek empire, Athens and Sparta
From Aphrodite to Zeus
There were many beliefs
And many great concepts
They prospered until 36 BC

But then the sun began to rise on a new era
When they, the Greeks, were defeated
Only 2000 years ago
By the Roman ranks and their amazing armies.

Ayub Mohamud (10)
Stockwell Primary School, Lambeth

My Monster

This is my monster, Izzy
She likes to eat
And she likes the heat
She likes to plant flowers
And likes to sleep for hours
She likes to wear a skirt
She also likes to wear a shirt
Izzy is pretty
And she is sometimes silly
Izzy is funny
And sometimes she is shy
At school, Izzy is learning about the law
Izzy is seven
Izzy has a brother called Bethan
She likes to read books
She loves to play with hooks
Izzy likes the colour pink
And she writes with ink
She likes to wear shoes with hearts.

Mellany Angel Vieira (7)
Stockwell Primary School, Lambeth

Lily The Tooth Fairy

Near a cocoon,
Where flowers bloomed,
Set at night where she takes flight.

As she dances and prances,
Through the night and as quiet as a mouse,
Tip-toes on the little girl's blouse,
As she shakes and trembles,
Turning blue, she looks under her pillow,
To find a shoe.

She was angry and cast a spell,
That the little girl would never have a tooth that fell.

Leena Omar Mohammed Ali (9)
Stockwell Primary School, Lambeth

The K9 Dog

The eager, elated dog was running around with a tennis ball
A K9 dog was mad, mean, malevolent, morbid and morose
It was attacking someone

The K9 saw a criminal
The criminal rapidly ran
In a rush, he got the criminal

Then the K9 dog became the world's best K9 dog ever
He lived happily ever after catching criminals.

Leonardo Ferreira (6)
Stockwell Primary School, Lambeth

Untitled

When I was 8
I would always play
With Ana and Sabrina
And help Miss B.

When I am 12
I will hang out with my new BFF.

When I'm 20
I will get a good job
Playing the piano.

When I am 28
I will play music till I die.

Erin Bohan (8)
Stockwell Primary School, Lambeth

Spring

S unflowers bloom in the sunlight
P ea pods burst
R unning through the dewy grass
I sla will find many birds singing
N o tree left bare
G limmering sun hiding in the trees.

Elijah Shipman (8)
Stockwell Primary School, Lambeth

The Wonders Of Space!

S tars shine bright in endless skies
P lanets twirl as galaxies rise
A steroids dance in cosmic streams
C omets blaze with fiery beams
E ternal void, yet full light.

Halima Begum (8)
Stockwell Primary School, Lambeth

Tigers

Tim the terrifying tiger
Tiptoes through tangled trees
His twitching tail thumping
His terrible teeth terrifying
Turtles
Who tumble away.

Shersy Encarnacion Arias (10)
Stockwell Primary School, Lambeth

It Is Nature

It is by nature soft as silk
A fluffy cloud as white as milk
Snow tops this tropical crop
The dirtiest part of a mop.

Matilde Correia (8)
Stockwell Primary School, Lambeth

Sharing Is Caring

I'm in the kitchen, whipping up a feast,
Veggies are what my sisters like the least,
I crack eggs and sift the flour,
Cream sugar and butter, for what seems like an hour.
Now it's time for me to stir in the milk,
Mixing the batter until it's smooth as silk,
Into the oven, it's time to bake,
Can you guess what I'm trying to make?
Ring, ring, ring sounds the alarm,
To my surprise, this recipe has worked a charm!
Out of the oven it's time to cool,
The smell in the air makes my sisters drool!
I slice the strawberries and whip the cream
I know this is going to taste like a dream,
This cake looks too good to eat,
And everyone is waiting for their treat!
My sisters think I'm being unfair!
Why you ask?
Because I won't share!
I made this cake and it's all mine,
Tough luck, girls, maybe next time!
Dad said I must share my cake,
So four big slices I shall make,

I watch as my sisters take huge greedy bites
The look on their faces is pure delight!
They all scream, "This is the best cake we've ever had!"
And I think to myself, *maybe sharing isn't so bad?*

Faith Leach (8)
Temple Sutton Primary School, Southend-On-Sea

Dreams

I go to bed and wait to sleep
Knowing magic adventure lies ahead
I shut my eyes, I close them tight
As I lie softly in my bed.

My special place, a world of dreams
Is my favourite place to be
Escape from school and boring work
And homework misery.

Where scary dragons roam, wild and free
And wizards cast their spell
Mermaids splash so innocently
And butterflies ring the bell.

Where angels sing and birds can talk
And trees speak out in joy
Where humpback whales fly through the breeze
A world humans can't destroy.

A world of creatures big and small
A place I call my home
Where kindness shines and fairness rules
A place you'll never feel alone.

Callum Armstrong (8)
Temple Sutton Primary School, Southend-On-Sea

Happy Hare

A girl is lonely and sad
She wants a friend real bad
She feels so downhearted and blue
She doesn't know what to do

She takes herself off for a walk
To find somebody to talk
She sits down in despair
Then sees a fluffy hare

The hare bounces up to the girl
Who holds out her hand
For the hare to smell
The hare bounds onto her knee
And she lets a shriek of glee

The happy hare and the happy girl
Go to a field to twirl and whirl
Now the girl is not lonely and sad anymore
Since she found a happy hare on the grassy floor.

Dolly Aylott (9)
Temple Sutton Primary School, Southend-On-Sea

Beautiful Rainforest

R ain dripping from the branch,
A s the branch blew in the wind,
I was there to see it all happen,
N oises to be heard all around me,
F rom droplets to birds chirping,
O h, how lovely it was,
R unning around as the wind swept my hair,
E njoying every second that passed by,
S lowly the rain started to slow down,
T hen all you heard was silence.

Evelyn-Ivy Poppy Button (9)
Temple Sutton Primary School, Southend-On-Sea

Sadness

Having no friends makes me sad,
Even the days go bad,
With nobody around,
No one to play with me.

A bee stings me,
As pain glides through my soul,
As my body burns like coal,
I have to cry.

To leave out all the pain,
As I scream through my jaw,
Asking for help,
With nobody around,
To look far out,
If I go out,
I won't be able to find my way.

Lillie Stemp (8)
Temple Sutton Primary School, Southend-On-Sea

Friendship

F unny times with my friends
R emarkable smile that never ends
I ncredible people they all are
E xcited laughter that goes far
N ice feelings they give me
D ynamite dancers, we will be
S mile and skipping all day long
H eartwarming sounds with our songs
I nspire me they all do
P ositive feeling, it's so true.

Victoria Ginn (8)
Temple Sutton Primary School, Southend-On-Sea

Winter Awakens

W inter awakens and autumn melts away
I cicles glisten in the morning sun
N umerous creatures hibernate in this season
T he snow is as soft as cotton and as fluffy as clouds,
E legant swans blend in with the picturesque scene,
R ivers make a clear, gentle melody while water flows through the placid river.

Nithika Selvakumar (9)
Temple Sutton Primary School, Southend-On-Sea

Every Animal

Some are tall
Some are small
Some live high
Some live low
Some can fly
Some can't
Every animal is amazing!
Monkeys, apes climb in trees
Cats and dogs sleep in cosy houses
Caterpillars to butterflies
Wolves at night howl to the sinister moon
Fish swim to the waving sea
Every animal is amazing!

Tola Grabowska (9)
Temple Sutton Primary School, Southend-On-Sea

Achieve To The Top

My school is my life
I achieve to drive
We read, we write
We think of our future bright
We learn to be kind not to leave them behind
We shout, we cry
But we never say bye
We study and play but never call it a day
Making friends through the way of every single day
Now I'm here in a great school in Essex.

Oscar Hainesborough (9)
Temple Sutton Primary School, Southend-On-Sea

The Mystery Light

I saw a flashing light
It appeared to be in my bookcase
But when I went to check
It automatically turned me to the right
I felt my hand reach out and I pulled
A book backwards
An exquisite ruby-red and black room
So I followed inside with curiosity
And I wonder and ponder
A secret mustn't be denied...

Ajla Malka (9)
Temple Sutton Primary School, Southend-On-Sea

I Like

I like sunshine.
I like rain.
I like flowers as they grow.
I like biscuits.
I like pancakes.
I like waffles when I wake.
I like dogs.
I like cats.
I like clowns in funny hats.
I like dancing in the rain.
I like flying in planes.
I like sleeping while it snows.
I like everything where I go.

Sadie Wavell (9)
Temple Sutton Primary School, Southend-On-Sea

Beautiful Game

F ootball is really fun
O ver the field
O bviously in the sun
T he time has come to score a goal
B ut will the keeper save the day?
A nd the crowd goes wild
L ily has scored a winning goal
"**L** et's all celebrate," Lily said.

William Smith (8)
Temple Sutton Primary School, Southend-On-Sea

Nature's Breeze

I feel a breeze
I know it's from the trees
It makes me freeze
Whilst blowing the leaves off the branches of the trees
It makes me feel cold and free.

I feel free from the breeze blowing in the trees,
Sailing down the river,
Feeling the wind of nature's breeze.

KC-Mylia Linggood (9)
Temple Sutton Primary School, Southend-On-Sea

Friends Forever

A friend is like a flower,
A violet to be exact,
Or maybe like a magnet that
Never becomes unattached,
A friend is like an owl,
Both friendly and brave.
A friend is like a spirit
That stays with you until the end.
What would we be if we did not have a friend?

Mia Rouse (9)
Temple Sutton Primary School, Southend-On-Sea

My Best Friend And Me

You bring joy to me
Everything I see belongs to me
Friendships are supposed to be happy
But mine is not.
You bring joy to me when I see you
Just like the roses when they bloom
Both of us are just like a path of love
But with roses
I just hope you understand.

Habibat Waheed (10)
Temple Sutton Primary School, Southend-On-Sea

The Twitter Tweeting Red Pandas

They twitter tweet from their mouths
The low quiet noises til south
I live in the bamboo forest
That is where you will see me eating my breakfast
I'm a member of the bear family
And you will find me very cuddly
I live in China
And I love my mama.

Evie-Rose Muller (8)
Temple Sutton Primary School, Southend-On-Sea

Best Friends

Flowers are like friends
Sweet and gentle
And when it feels like
The raining teardrops will
Never stop, they will soak
The tears up and brighten
Your day up
So when you cry, they're
Always nearby to hug
Them dry.

Ofelia Dean (8)
Temple Sutton Primary School, Southend-On-Sea

Fat Cat

Hi, my name is Matt
Have I told you about my fat cat?
One day there was a fat cat which sat on a mat
Which had a picture of a rat
Which wore a black hat.
The owner known as Fat Man
Adopted a cat and saw Bruno the dog playing Uno.

Dominic Smith (10)
Temple Sutton Primary School, Southend-On-Sea

Cute Animals

A nimals are so interesting
N octurnal is nightly
I nsects are animals
M ammals come in different sizes
A nimals eat other animals
L ife span varies
S mall animals are so, so cute.

Vinnie Wright (9)
Temple Sutton Primary School, Southend-On-Sea

Spring

As winter dies and spring rises,
Butterflies come out to play,
Bees hiving the beautiful flowers,
Green leaves approaching on the treetops,
Bunnies hopping around happily on the fields,
I love spring and so should you.

Sienna O'Neill (9)
Temple Sutton Primary School, Southend-On-Sea

My School, My Life

Where we have a wonderful ride
We spell, we write
We make our future shine bright
We love, not hate
We skip through the gates
We learn to respect
Never neglect
That's what we call my school, my life.

Ria Simpson (9)
Temple Sutton Primary School, Southend-On-Sea

Sloths

S loths are fascinating,
L iving creatures in their fur
O n their own, travelling
T rekking through the rainforest
H anging upside down
S lowly moving from branch to branch.

Kleisa Kaloshi (8)
Temple Sutton Primary School, Southend-On-Sea

Fire

F ire, fire, quick, get away quickly. *Bang! Ah!*
I f there is a fire in the building, get to shelter quickly
R emember always be safe when there is a fire
E njoy, I hope you like my poem.

Isabella Jo Ann Lew (8)
Temple Sutton Primary School, Southend-On-Sea

Panda!

P owerful and fierce
A cute teddy bear
N ibbles on bamboo
D enning in hollowed-out caves
A beautiful creature.

Sunny Li (8)
Temple Sutton Primary School, Southend-On-Sea

Food Cycle

There is so much food I haven't tried
It all looks so good
But my tummy is fully occupied
I'm so full, I'm in a bad mood
It's like my tastebuds have died

But uh-oh this feeling is new
I really think I need the loo
I won't say what I need to do!

Freddie Fletcher (8)
The New Beacon School, Sevenoaks

As I Grow Up

As I grow up, the seasons begin to change
I get older, nothing gets better
I don't want to grow up as I get older
I have to be more mature
I have more responsibilities
I don't want to grow up
I watch time pass
I wish I could live forever
I don't want to grow up
As I grow up, things begin to change
I realise this change might not be that bad
I don't want to grow up
I live alone
I miss my family
I don't want to grow up.

Isabella Jackson (8)
Thorpe Primary School, Idle

Summertime

Summer can be hot
People can burn up
The leaves are bright green
In summer it can be rainy sometimes
But when it's summer
Most of the time it's bright and warm
People can play games like tig
Or hide-and-seek and more
Summer can be fun if you like it or not
In summer, sometimes you can get ice cream
Which can cool you down
You can hear the birds tweeting
And the sound of lawnmowers
At the crack of dawn.

Bella-Mai B (8)
Thorpe Primary School, Idle

Four Seasons

Spring, summer, autumn, winter,
Our four seasons,
Summer and winter,
Summer has sun, but winter hasn't any,
Animals come out to play in spring,
In autumn, they hide away,
Autumn leaves fall,
Red, orange and yellow,
But Halloween's no reason to be mellow,
In winter, there's cheer,
And in autumn, there is fright,
Spring has pillowy petals,
In summer, dandelion clocks take flight.

Anaya Shah (9)
Thorpe Primary School, Idle

A Worm That Never Used To Wiggle

The worm tried and tried
But still couldn't do it
He cried and cried
But he still couldn't do it
But then one day he had one steady wiggle
The next day he had another steady wiggle
He was so happy, that he even tried again
He improved every day
His friends were proud of him
The next morning he could wiggle
From then on he lived his best life
With friends and family.

Anishah Eqbal (9)
Thorpe Primary School, Idle

Nature Is Everywhere

Nature is everywhere
Nature is everywhere you go
Everything that lives and grows is nature
Animals, big and small
Nature is beautiful in every way
Nature is wonderful, exciting and needs our care
So listen, learn and do your part
To keep our beautiful nature
And don't forget
Nature is a very important part
Of our lives.

Isabel Waite (8)
Thorpe Primary School, Idle

The Park Is Dark

The park is so dark
I can't see a thing
I hope nothing is under my feet
Do you know what is under my feet?
There is something under my feet!
What is it?

Natalie Greaves (8)
Thorpe Primary School, Idle

Halloween Night

Autumn is Halloween - when children ask for sweets,
When I knock on a door,
A colourful candy from the bowl screams my name,
As I walk,
Orange leaves fly through the air,
Rustling about until it lands gently on the leafy ground,
Once I arrive at my house,
I pile all of my candy together,
And then, I eat them with hot chocolate.

As vibrant leaves get pushed away by the trees,
Squirrels jump out of their homes and gather nuts to prepare for the winter,
As Halloween comes,
People decorate their houses and make them spooky with pumpkins,
When the sun falls.
Night comes and people go knocking on doors asking for candy,
When it starts to get cold,
Birds fly,
While squirrels work hard like miners.

Spiky, green conkers that attach to your clothes are looking for their next victim,
The lanterns blast into the sky,
Shining every night,
The sticks I step on make a *crunch! Crisp! Crack!* Noise,
And it gives me a tingly feeling,
When I look into the sky,
I absorb the round moon, giving me a little wink.

Kaiden Kelly (9)
Woodstock Primary School, Leicester

Autumn Time

The warm hug of summer loosens its grip
The whole world has a sensory song
A season full of light and celebration
My heart is beating with joy and popcorn and movie night.

The cold hug of autumn tightens its grip
The whole world is a sensory song
Light and celebration
My heart beats with joy and popcorn.

We hear tweets of birds
We smell food and trees
Leaves fall onto the ground, heavy
The sun shines like gold and silver in the sky
It tastes like cotton candy.

We went to see the fireworks
The earth shook like rocks
The squeak of humans were screaming
Little children were playing on the playground
The sun was as lovely as a golden ruby in the sky.

We went to see the celebration
People everywhere squealing like squirrels everywhere.

Marlvin Ndlovu (8)
Woodstock Primary School, Leicester

Autumn Is Finally Here

We run inside the house, and turn on the radiator,
Close all the windows and turn the heating on,
Summer loosens its grip, we run and get our pyjamas on,
And grab blankets.

Now it's getting cold, we can have the fire on,
And getting into the cold, candy cane warm,
The orange, yellow and red leaves fall down on our roof,
Giving me the autumn spirit.

The autumn weather is full of joy,
Happiness cuddles and warm is what we need,
We have brown candy canes and hot chocolate,
We bake cookies.

Now it's night-time, we snuggle the way while the sun goes away,
We sleep the way and have random dreams.
We wake up, run downstairs, have warm hot chocolate,
We run onto the sofa and drink our hot chocolate.

Ava Connely (8)
Woodstock Primary School, Leicester

Autumn Is Here

Autumn is Halloween,
Snickers and Bounty are calling my name!
Halloween is spooky and fun,
The pumpkins are as bright as the sun

The trees dry up like water in a bottle,
The ruby-red golden leaves as hot as the sun.
Stars as hot as the sun just like the Earth's core.
In autumn there are a lot of fog and puddles.

The leaves fall down as the sun shines,
How silently they tumble down and come to rest upon the ground.
The wind is playing autumn games,
The leaves fly until they reach the ground.

The rain covers the leaves as the wind blows,
The rain cries until the leaves fly.
The rain drips while the puddles splash,
The rain giggles while the road fills with water.

Zohaib Shah (8)
Woodstock Primary School, Leicester

Autumn Time

Autumn is Halloween and Bonfire Night
And sweets call my name.
Halloween is spooky and fun.
The pumpkins are big and fun to carve.

The rusty gold leaves dancing
And the sun shining while the children are smiling
And the wind sings as loud as it can.
The trees hide from the squirrels.

The lanterns are like a glowing moon.
The leaves are silent as they tumble down as they rest.
The wind is playing autumn games.
At other times, they wildly fly until they reach the sky.

The water drops and the trees move.
The path giggles as the tree tells jokes.
The sun shines bright.
The rain cries while the trees sing.

Beau Mitchell (9)
Woodstock Primary School, Leicester

Untitled

The sweet taste of pumpkin pie is calling my name.
I walk all around the streets and knock on doors so I get the mouth-watering candy.
Halloween is a time of screaming and laughter.
The russet red trees stand tall with you laughing and giggling.
The golden gem of the sun shifts upon the trees and streets,
The leaves as red as a lethal eclipse.
Autumn is supercalifragilisticexpialidocious.
Berries are red, juicy and ready to pick.
The wild wind swerves around the trees.

At midnight the colourful mystic fireworks burst into laughter and leave people amazed.
In the field there is a long, thick piece of mist and it makes everything disappear.

Harvi Parvaga (8)
Woodstock Primary School, Leicester

Bonfire Night And Halloween

Autumn is for Halloween and Bonfire Night.
Licking lovely lollipops.
Stick toffee apples are sweet like cotton candy.
Fireworks burst when they are angry.

Bright colours of leaves smile at me.
The colours look like a rainbow that shines on the floor.
I kick the leaves, laughing like my sister.

Squirrels dance in the rain.
Conkers with shiny jewels inside them.
Leaves fall, bringing joy to our land.
Birds tweet in harmony.

Fireworks *pop* and *bang!*
Birds tweet, bringing joy.
People scream from the fireworks.
I laugh because I'm having fun!

Mya Gregory (8)
Woodstock Primary School, Leicester

What Autumn Is Like

Autumn is Bonfire Night and Halloween,
While I was doing Halloween, sweets were calling my name,
So that could be collected.
Fireworks were calling me, so they could be used and exploded!

The ruby red leaves were falling off the trees,
All of them were preparing for their goodbyes,
While they were falling off the dry tree.

The squirrel ran like an Olympian for the nuts and conkers,
So it could have a tasty dinner,
The tree waved at the leaves,
The leaves were crunching and cracking,
Because it was autumn.
The leaves changed to a ruby-red colour,
Because it was autumn.

Freddie Beeching-Townsend (8)
Woodstock Primary School, Leicester

Fireworks

Autumn is fireworks. *Pop, bang*, explode.
Fireworks burst into laughter.

The golden leaves fall off the tree as they say goodbye.
The ruby-red leaves turn as they fall off.
Golden leaves dance as they go left and right.
The wind rushes and whooshes.

The squirrels are dancing in the rain.
The leaves tumble down as they rest.
The leaves *crisp, crunch, crack* as they get to the ground.
The wind is playing autumn games.

The leaves cry as the tree sings.
The wind whooshes.
The wind spins around.
The leaves fall to the ground.

Nimrat Kaur (8)
Woodstock Primary School, Leicester

Autumn Time

Autumn is a sensory season, full of light and celebration.
Autumn absorbs heat and makes it cold.
Collecting brown, shiny conkers, kicking leaves.
The underfoot crunch, crisp sound.

All around, you see orange leaves.
It is now dark as autumn rises.
Red leaves now flutter down and change.
Pumpkins glow in the night.

Bonfire night and fireworks.
Costumes getting bought.
Fires are lit.
Families with popcorn and watching TV.

You smell spicy food.
Sweets flow through the air.
Cotton candy takes the air.
The smell of tea.

Kingsley Baptiste (8)
Woodstock Primary School, Leicester

Love Autumn

Autumn is Diwali,
Fireworks *sizzle! Crack! Pop!*
Fireworks burst into the sky with vivid colours,
Fireworks are as loud as thunder,
Squirrels dance in the rain,
Many sweets are calling my name,
Golden leaves dance away from the other side,
The squirrels climb from the bushy trees,
Spiky conkers are like tennis balls,
Leaves dance away from the trees,
The sun hides behind the enormous trees,
Squirrels run with acorns,
Their mouths full,
Pumpkins glowing like scary demons,
Birds whistle like humans.

Jaden Tandel (8)
Woodstock Primary School, Leicester

Autumn

Autumn is a warm hug,
Turning colder and colder until it's freezing.
Dropping their treasures for passers-by,
To the conker tree to collect its treasures.

The crunching sounds from underfoot,
My heart full of anticipation,
A warm hug from nature.

My heart is full of movie nights and popcorn,
Jumping with joy and happiness.
The sound makes me cheer the loudest,
Makes me fear, in the festive cheer.

The smells make me think of noodles
And more tasty things,
Mesmerising the foods.

Mohammed Sulaimon (8)
Woodstock Primary School, Leicester

Untitled

I hate autumn, I wish it wasn't a thing
I don't like it
I would rather go to school than be in autumn
I don't like it
I don't want do it
I want to go to school
I want to get away from it
And never do it again
No, I want it to just always be summer
It would be sick
I will love it
School holiday, school holiday
I hate autumn

I can't even wait to go on trips and have fun
But no, I stay in
Horrible weather, stay indoors
No football all because of stupid autumn.

Mohamed Osman (8)
Woodstock Primary School, Leicester

Autumn Sky

As we sit down watching the sky, the fireworks fly
As we open the windows... *bang, pop* it screams
As the morning comes, we walk outside thinking about last night

As we walk along the leaves, we see bare trees
Kids finding conkers as we look for pumpkins for Halloween
The sun sleeps, our town sleeps as we walk home

I walk through the corridor
Rusty leaves running through the wind
I walk outside, leaves fall from the sky
Lanterns laugh as I walk past
As I walk, colourful leaves rush through.

Iman Siyad (8)
Woodstock Primary School, Leicester

Autumn Time!

Autumn is the dream,
I love autumn hats and gloves.
Autumn is November,
Dark nights,
The warm hugs
Give a hug to everyone.

My hats hug me tight,
I love autumn.
It's fireworks banging,
Skipping in the leaves
And jumping high in the sky.

Pumpkins and costumes and lights,
I love it,
Great trees lack and treat
And cold in the sky.

Those generous trees,
In clutter of all.
Sit back and rest and sing,
Autumn is here,
I love autumn,
Autumn stay!

Paigan Goulty (8)
Woodstock Primary School, Leicester

Autumn's Coming

The warm hug of summer loosens its grip,
Collecting conkers, kicking leaves,
Autumn is the cold hug.
The sensory season full of light.

The whole world is a sensory song.
People start the celebration.
People stay inside
When I play outside.

The cold wind blows,
The trees start waving,
Conkers fall like rain,
The tree decorated with red and green.

People set off fireworks,
I listen to it scream,
Or I watch colours explode,
I stay at the radiator.

Shevin Geekianage (8)
Woodstock Primary School, Leicester

Autumn

Autumn is my birthday,
It is ten days after Halloween.
Fireworks fill my mind with warm and vivid colours,
Chocolate, sweets, toffee apples call my name.

Russet ruby-red leaves lie on the floor,
Deep inside my hat and scarf, I smile.
Collecting conkers, kicking leaves,
Vivid leaves lie on the floor.

Vivid colours light up the sky on Bonfire Night,
The wind is playing autumn games.
Footsteps land on leaves, crunching, crisp, crackling,
The wind whistles.

Oscar Smyth (8)
Woodstock Primary School, Leicester

Untitled

Autumn is Bonfire Night,
Fireworks calling my name to go about in the darkness.
Fireworks dashing and whooshing into the darkness.
Sizzle! Bang! Pop! Crackle!

Ruby-red dry leaves dancing from the trees.
Fireworks whooshing and dashing up into the sky.
The squirrels dancing on the autumnal, dry, crunchy leaves.
The waterfall dashes to the end of the waterfall.

The wind playing tag in the country leaves,
The squirrels blending in trees.

Redeen Mahmood (8)
Woodstock Primary School, Leicester

Autumn Time!

Autumn is here
The warm hug of summer loosens its grip
Now time to go to the conker tree
I collect the tree's treasure

It gets colder, mistier, darker
Leaves fall off the tree, different colours
With children knocking at my door

There are fireworks
People with joy
I am opening the door, giving sweets out
Yummy, *bang, fizz*

I can smell pumpkin spice lattes
I can smell soup
I can smell burning fireworks.

Courtney Howkins (8)
Woodstock Primary School, Leicester

Autumn

Autumn is home
When it's autumn, I like to get cosy in my bed
And drink hot chocolate
The hot chocolate is calling my name!
Sometimes, when I go outside for fresh air,
I step in a pile of crunching, cracking leaves,
Bright colours of leaves dancing on paths,
The colours look bright and beautiful all together.

Squirrels dancing in the rain,
Conkers with shiny jewels inside them,
Leaves falling, bringing joy to our land,
Ruby, russet leaves shouting
As they want to be looked at.

Bilal Youssouf (8)
Woodstock Primary School, Leicester

Autumn

Autumn is full of lights and celebration,
My heart is full of anticipation,
Bonfire Night and Diwali are lights and celebration,
Autumn creeps when the leaves fall.

It is getting colder, all the leaves fall,
It changes colour and goes darker,
I need my coat,
I love autumn.

I taste the angry spice,
I taste samosas,
I can taste hot chocolate,
I can't help the taste!

As Diwali leaves,
Autumn creeps again,
All the leaves are crunching,
Deep in autumn clothes.

Anaya Chauhan (9)
Woodstock Primary School, Leicester

Autumn Time!

Autumn is a warm nice season
The best is having a movie night
Popcorn smell in the air
Staying up late and drinking hot chocolate

Autumn looks like fun
My heart is full with things to do
To go out and play in the leaves to go in
We go home and eat food

We go home
Turning on the heating and getting in pyjamas
And wash our hands and get in bed
And watch TV and watch the seasons.

Skyler Wall-Finnemore (9)
Woodstock Primary School, Leicester

Untitled

Autumn is trees waving goodbye to the leaves
As the wind blows away the leaves
And trees waving their last goodbye
As leaves fall off the trees
Glowing, brilliant autumn sun
Berries, red and black, ready to pick and eat

In autumn the damp grass waves
The wind blows and whistles
As the trees wave in the woods
As you walk through the leaves
You can hear the cracking and crunching.

Khortez-Azzi Seare (8)
Woodstock Primary School, Leicester

Autumn Morning

Autumn is the wet hug of November,
Collecting orange leaves,
The day that came,
The time of candy nights.

The time for pillow fights,
The beautiful colour orange,
Candy apple on the table,
Autumn turns into winter.

The long, brown hills we tumble down,
Thin, long branches,
Bright, yellow sun,
Blue, beautiful sky.

Birds squawk - they know it's time for autumn,
Rain swimming down,
The wind coming down,
The green slowly going.

Lehat Ibrahim (8)
Woodstock Primary School, Leicester

Untitled

Autumn is wet and cold weather,
When we shake the trees, the leaves fall off,
Like a snake shedding its skin,
The leaves are orange, red and green,
The cold makes me want hot chocolate,
In autumn, the damp soggy rain makes slippery puddles fun to jump in,
The frosty, crunchy leaves have been thrown out to die,
The mist howls like a ghost,
The lazy sun is a colourful diamond.

Bentley Thompson (8)
Woodstock Primary School, Leicester

Untitled

In autumn the leaves shake
When you walk through the leaves
They crunch like a bag of crisps
The berries are shiny like a beautiful ruby
The leaves are colourful

In autumn the fog is like a ghost
The cold tingles my nose, toes and fingers
I love to drink hot chocolate
The leaves wave goodbye to the trees.

Kazirie Morgan (8)
Woodstock Primary School, Leicester

Bonfire Night

Autumn is Bonfire Night,
Sizzling sausages that make your mouth water.

Fireworks explode like sparks of fire,
Pop pop! Bang bang! Sss pop!

The leaves fall from side to side,
Squirrels eating acorns on trees.

Raindrops falling in puddles,
Hearing birds sing through the wind.

Praise Iyobosa Ekhase (8)
Woodstock Primary School, Leicester

Autumn Is Here

We run in and turn on the radiator
We get all undressed
And grab a blanket
Hop on the couch.

Now that it's autumn
It is getting cold and rainy
The sky is getting grey
And the trees are misty

In autumn
It is rainy and it snows.

Star Cassidy (8)
Woodstock Primary School, Leicester

YOUNG WRITERS INFORMATION

We hope you have enjoyed reading this book – and that you will continue to in the coming years.

If you're the parent or family member of an enthusiastic poet or story writer, do visit our website **www.youngwriters.co.uk/subscribe** and sign up to receive news, competitions, writing challenges and tips, activities and much, much more! There's lots to keep budding writers motivated!

If you would like to order further copies of this book, or any of our other titles, then please give us a call or order via your online account.

Young Writers
Remus House
Coltsfoot Drive
Peterborough
PE2 9BF
(01733) 890066
info@youngwriters.co.uk

Join in the conversation!
Tips, news, giveaways and much more!

YoungWritersUK   YoungWritersCW

youngwriterscw   youngwriterscw